The Whole Story

Christina Hart-Davies is well known for her precise and accurate botanical watercolours, which feature in prestigious collections worldwide and have won many awards including six RHS Gold medals, most recently in 2018. She has been commissioned several times to illustrate field guides to Britain's wildflowers, most notably the *Collins Flower Guide*. Christina graduated in Typography & Graphic Communication from the University of Reading and her design background is invaluable in her illustration work and influences the composition of her exhibition paintings. She is an experienced and popular tutor and enjoys encouraging people to find their own style in which to celebrate plants of all kinds.

www.christinahartdavies.co.uk

Botanical Art Portfolios

Botanical Art Portfolios is a new series featuring distinguished botanical artists, their work and their inspiration. Intentionally both beautiful and useful, these handy-sized paperbacks are designed to be taken anywhere, referred to, collected and gazed at. Each book will bring out the personality of its individual artist, showcase their work and share why they love what they do, explain their choice of subjects, the distinct techniques they have developed, and their failures as well as their successes. The series is edited by Julia Trickey, an internationally-acclaimed botanical artist and tutor. She has been awarded four RHS gold medals and exhibited all over the world.

See tworiverspress.com/about/botanical-art-portfolios for more information.

Also published by Two Rivers Press

The Art & History of Whiteknights edited by Jenny Halstead
The Art of Peter Hay by John Froy with Martin Andrews
Bonjour Mr Inshaw by Peter Robinson & David Inshaw
Botanical Artistry by Julia Trickey
The Greenwood Trees: History, folklore and uses of Britain's trees by Christina Hart-Davies
Reading Abbey and the Abbey Quarter by Peter Durrant and John Painter
Reading's Bayeux Tapestry by Reading Museum
A Coming of Age: Celebrating 18 Years of Botanical Painting by the Eden Project Florilegium Society by Ros Franklin
A Wild Plant Year: History, folklore and uses of Britain's flora by Christina Hart-Davies
Silchester: Life on the Dig by Jenny Halstead & Michael Fulford
Caught on Camera: Reading in the 70s by Terry Allsop
Plant Portraits by Post: Post & Go British Flora by Julia Trickey
Allen W. Seaby: Art and Nature by Martin Andrews & Robert Gillmor
Cover Birds by Robert Gillmor
An Artist's Year in the Harris Garden by Jenny Halstead
Caversham Court Gardens: A Heritage Guide by Friends of Caversham Court Gardens
Birds, Blocks & Stamps: Post & Go Birds of Britain by Robert Gillmor
Down by the River: The Thames and Kennet in Reading by Gillian Clark

The Whole Story

Painting more than just the flowers

Christina Hart-Davies

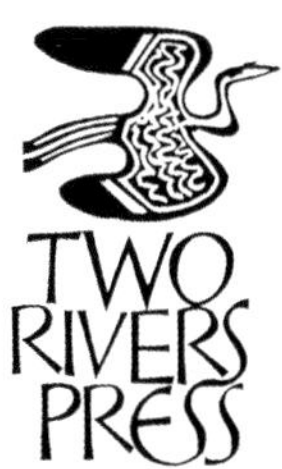

TWO RIVERS PRESS

First published in the UK in 2020 by Two Rivers Press
7 Denmark Road, Reading RG1 5PA
www.tworiverspress.com

© Two Rivers Press 2020
© in text and artwork Christina Hart-Davies 2020

ISBN 978-1-909747-63-0

1 2 3 4 5 6 7 8 9

Two Rivers Press is represented in the UK by Inpress Ltd and distributed by NBNi.

Cover painting by Christina Hart-Davies: *Ramalina fastigiata* and other lichens

Cover design by Nadja Guggi
Text design by Nadja Guggi and typeset in Parisine

Printed and bound in Great Britain by Gomer Press, Ceredigion

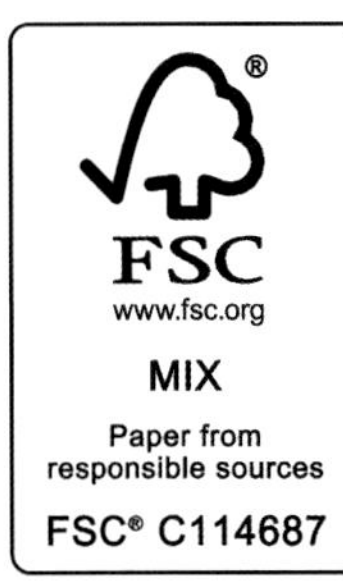

Acknowledgements

I am indebted to Myles Archibald at HarperCollins for permission to reproduce the Roses plate from *Collins Flower Guide*, published in 2009. The second edition, renamed *Collins Wild Flower Guide*, was published in 2016. My thanks also go to those people who own some of the paintings reproduced in this book.

Throughout my long career I have received help and encouragement from botanists, field naturalists, artists, students, writers, teachers, storytellers and friends too numerous to mention individually. I deeply appreciate you all. My special thanks go to Jo, Sally and Paul for their unstinting support.

My thanks go to the staff at Two Rivers Press, especially to Sally Mortimore and Nadja Guggi, for once again making my text and paintings into a beautiful book. As I near the end of my painting career, this will be a fitting retrospective, which I hope will interest and inspire others in the future.

Note

For current laws on picking wild plants consult the Botanical Society of Britain and Ireland (www.bsbi.org.uk) and look for the downloadable BSBI Code of Conduct.

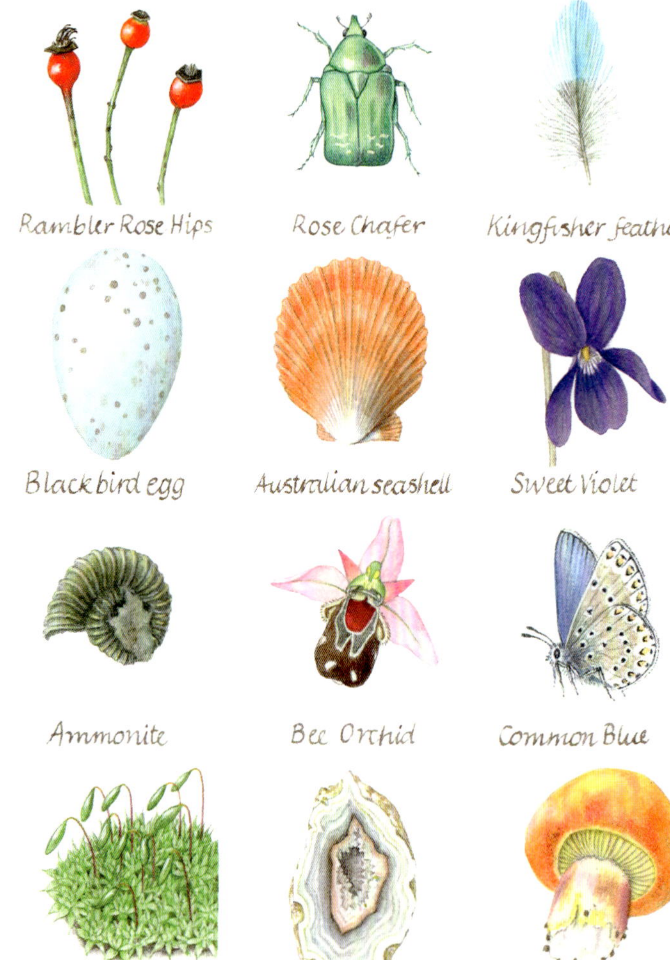

Rambler Rose Hips	Rose Chafer	Kingfisher feather
Black bird egg	Australian seashell	Sweet Violet
Ammonite	Bee Orchid	Common Blue
Mnium hornum	Geode	'Plums & Custard'

Contents

Opposite page:
Nature's Little Treasures

The whole story

This book is entitled *The Whole Story,* because I believe that the beauty of flowers is only part of the picture. Plants do not grow in isolation but in a habitat: they are surrounded by other species and may interact with them. They may depend upon certain insects for pollination, or be attacked by creatures or diseases. They go through different stages of development and decay. They may have close relatives. Humans may have used them for a multitude of purposes, studied their scientific properties, given them nicknames or woven legends about them. All these factors reveal more about a plant than simply what it looks like, and I enjoy telling more of the whole story in my work.

What brought me here?

For a botanical artist, I had a very fortunate start. My mother had been a fashion designer before World War II, so drawing and design were always part of my life, perhaps even in my genes. My father was interested in everything and encouraged a similar curiosity in me. Living in a small country town, my friends and I spent our time, as children did in those days, playing in the fields or walking to school unaccompanied. We became familiar with wild plants and even used them in our games. I can remember, aged five or six, picking the pale, pastel petals from yarrow flowers and scattering them over playmates (and strangers!) as 'confetti'. When my parents got their first car, Sunday drives and country picnics deepened my connection with the natural world. I became a major contributor to the class nature table. My painting is still driven by that fascination with all things natural and the ways in which they interact.

Forced at school to choose between arts and sciences, I opted for the arts route. Eventually I graduated with a degree in Typography and Graphic Communication. My design background has been invaluable throughout

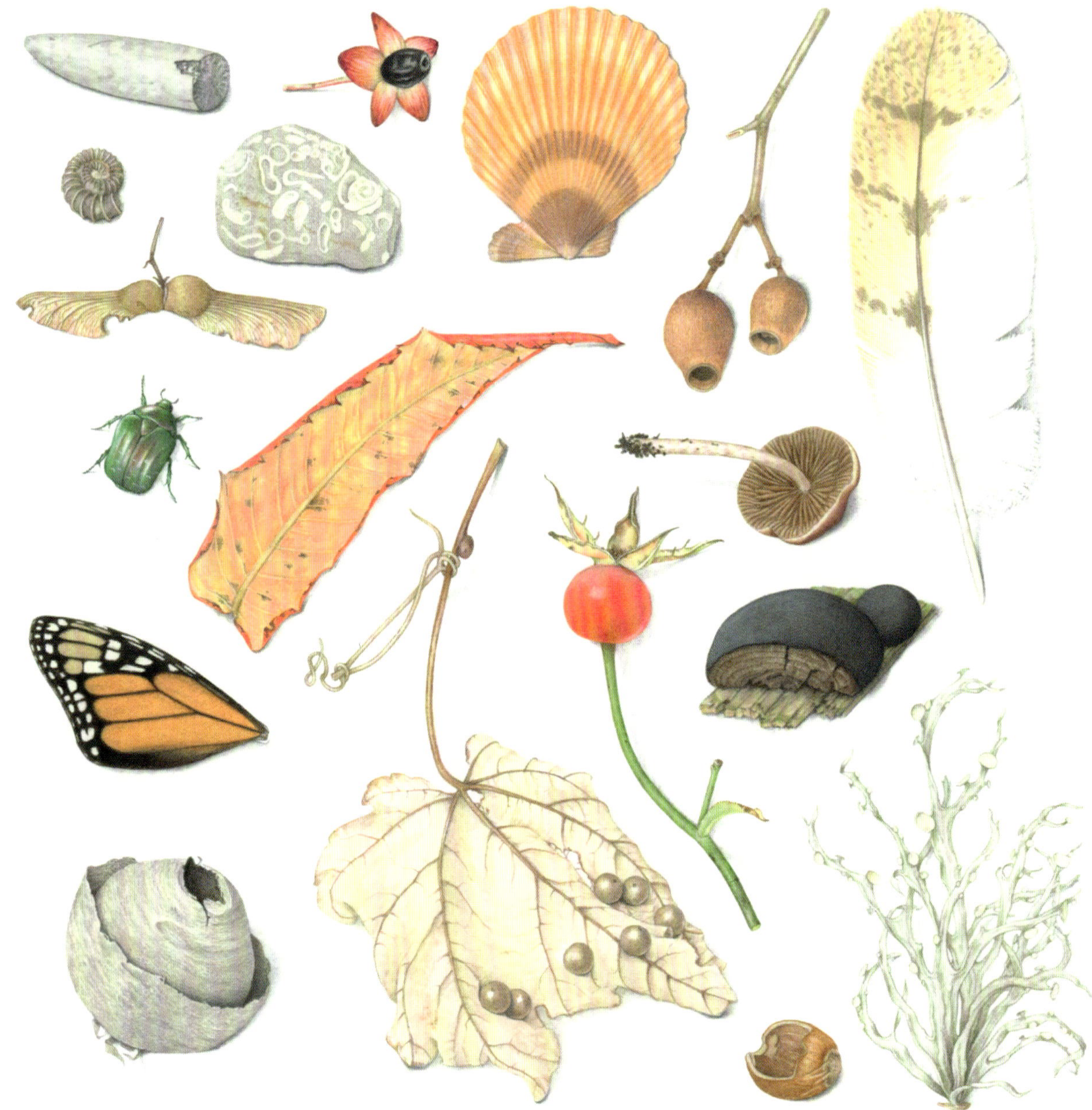

my career, both in art and illustration. In the 1970s, I moved to Dorset and began painting plants: first as a hobby, then as a living. Illustration work began to build up, and at the same time there were galleries and exhibitions to supply. Most important of all the exhibitions were the Royal Horticultural Society (RHS) shows in London, where work is judged and awarded medals. I first showed there in 1981.

I enjoyed painting miniatures and served on the council of the Hilliard Society of Miniaturists as well as that of the Royal Society of Miniature Painters, Sculptors and Gravers (RMS). Suzanne Lucas, President of the RMS at the time, was concerned about the lack of respect accorded to plant painting by most art societies. She proposed the foundation of a new society – the Society of Botanical Artists (SBA) – dedicated to botanical art in all its forms, and I was honoured (and terrified!) when she asked me to be its first honorary secretary. I served the SBA in that capacity for its first ten years.

Teaching is a joy to me too. I have had a lot of help and advice from other artists, and it feels only right to pass on what I can. It is very rewarding to encourage others to find and develop their style, enabling them to derive as much pleasure from the genre as I do.

I love teaching, painting and illustrating, but doing all three at the same time has sometimes been challenging. Now I have reached what seems to be a happy balance, and I will keep going for as long as I am able. Botanical painting is a wonderful synthesis of art and science and, for me, often combines with history and folklore too – 'the whole story', in fact.

Blackberry, watercolour on vellum,
actual size

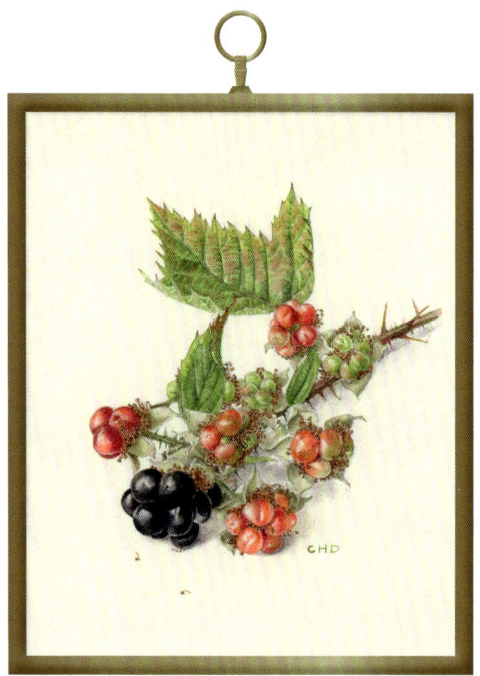

Blackberry miniature

Miniatures were originally intended to be held in the hand, providing an intimate connection with the subject. I love this way of working and find vellum is the perfect medium. It allows crisp detail, but with a beautiful translucence. The trick is not to use the paint too wet or too thick. This painting was shown at an RMS exhibition in London in the 1980s.

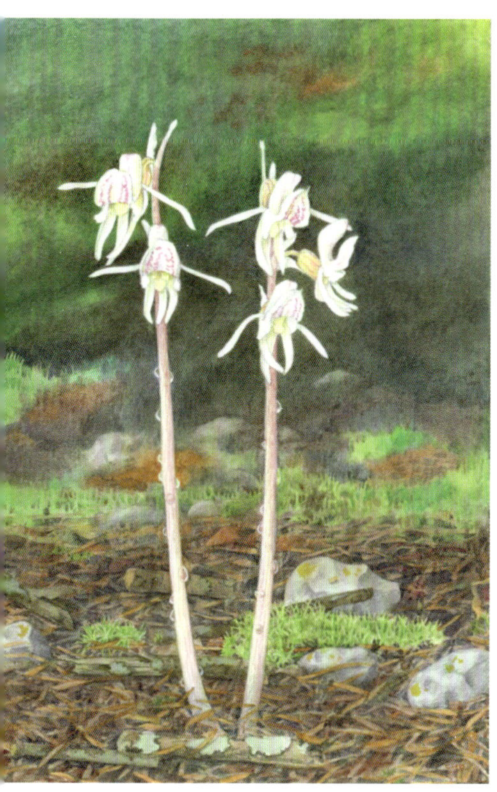

Ghost orchid *Epipogium aphyllum*

Art or illustration?

People often ask about the difference between botanical art and botanical illustration. To me, the difference lies in the essential purpose of the painting or drawing. Art is made primarily to *celebrate* a plant, while an illustration is intended primarily to *explain* it. There are, of course, huge overlaps: illustrations can be beautiful; art can be scientifically accurate. At a more practical level, illustrations are normally commissioned by authors or publishers for specific purposes and to given formats, while art is usually the painter's own choice of subject and treatment. This is not to denigrate either end of the spectrum. Each is a serious and valid way of portraying subjects.

My career has straddled both, and they each have advantages and drawbacks. When working on a long illustration project, I miss the freedom of making exhibition paintings. On the other hand, I do enjoy the rigour and challenge of illustration: it makes me paint subjects I might not otherwise consider, and I learn about and appreciate them more.

Ghost orchid

This elusive saprophytic orchid was declared extinct in Britain in 2005 after not having been recorded for many years. In 2009 it reappeared in a new site but, at time of writing, has not been seen since. This painting was based on sketches and photographs I made in France. I included the dark woodland habitat to give the pallid plant a background. In illustrations for identification guides I have to show it isolated on white, but to make it show up well enough for reproduction, it needs a strong holding line around the edge.

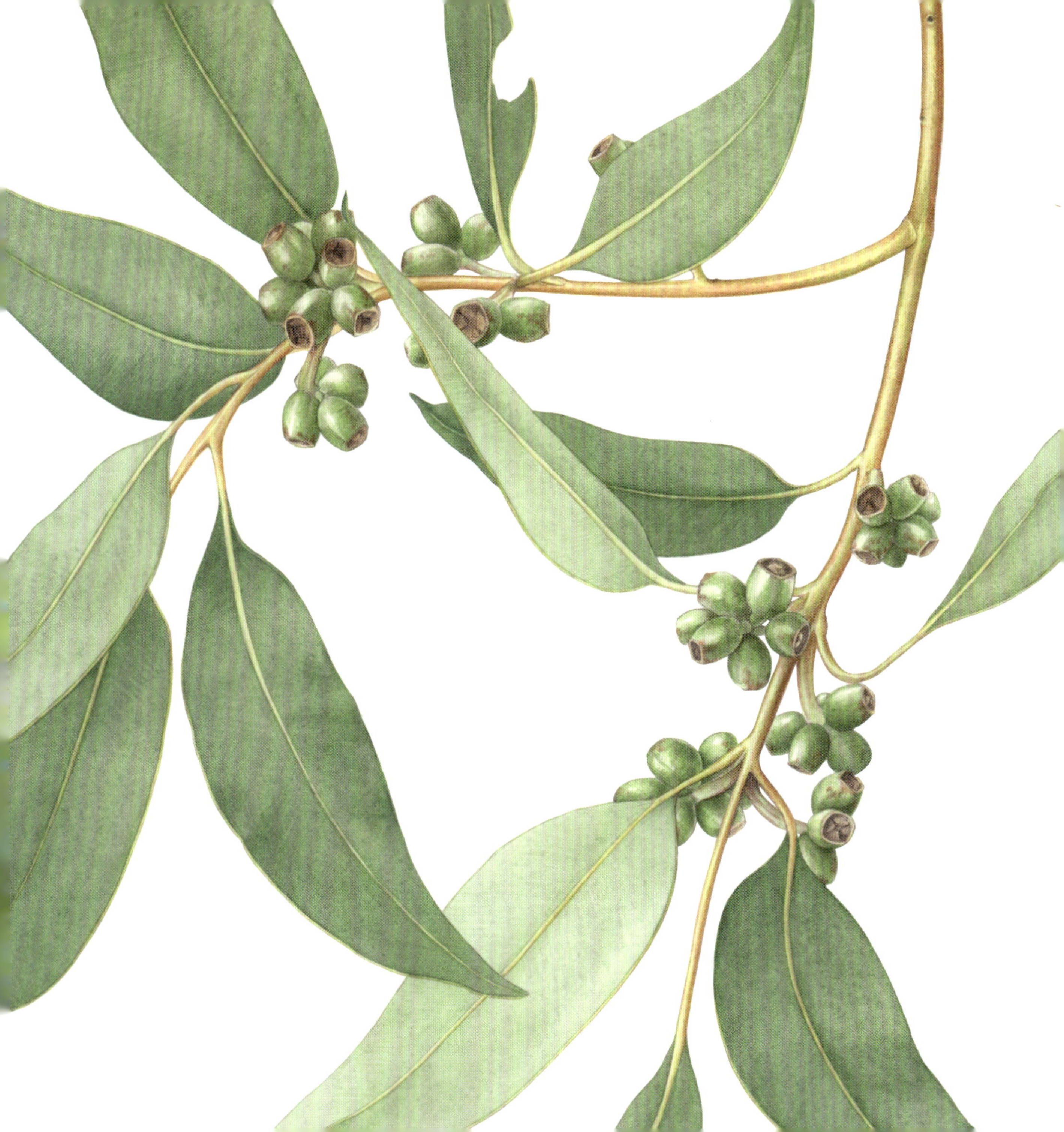

Section 1
The plants

The plants

British native plants

I love painting the rich and beautiful native flora of Britain. As an illustrator I have had to paint a wide variety of subjects – anything from hands using secateurs to the genitalia of a micro-moth – but luckily, the British flora has often been the required subject, too. Several of these illustrations are shown here, along with exhibition paintings.

Rosebay willowherb

I have always had a soft spot for this plant and remember being beguiled by its swathes of glorious colour as a child: there were still bomb sites in those days, and it flourishes on burnt ground (hence its other name, 'fireweed'). It was one of the first plants whose name I learned.

This painting was shown in the English exhibition organised as part of the first Botanical Art Worldwide event in 2018. I chose this subject as it is both well-known and beautifully striking, and it has a clear connection to part of our recent history. I decided to paint the colourful, flowering spike but to render the fruiting spike in pencil, which suits the lightness of the seeds with their pappae parachutes. I especially like the way the seeds are so neatly packed into the long pods before floating free once the pods open.

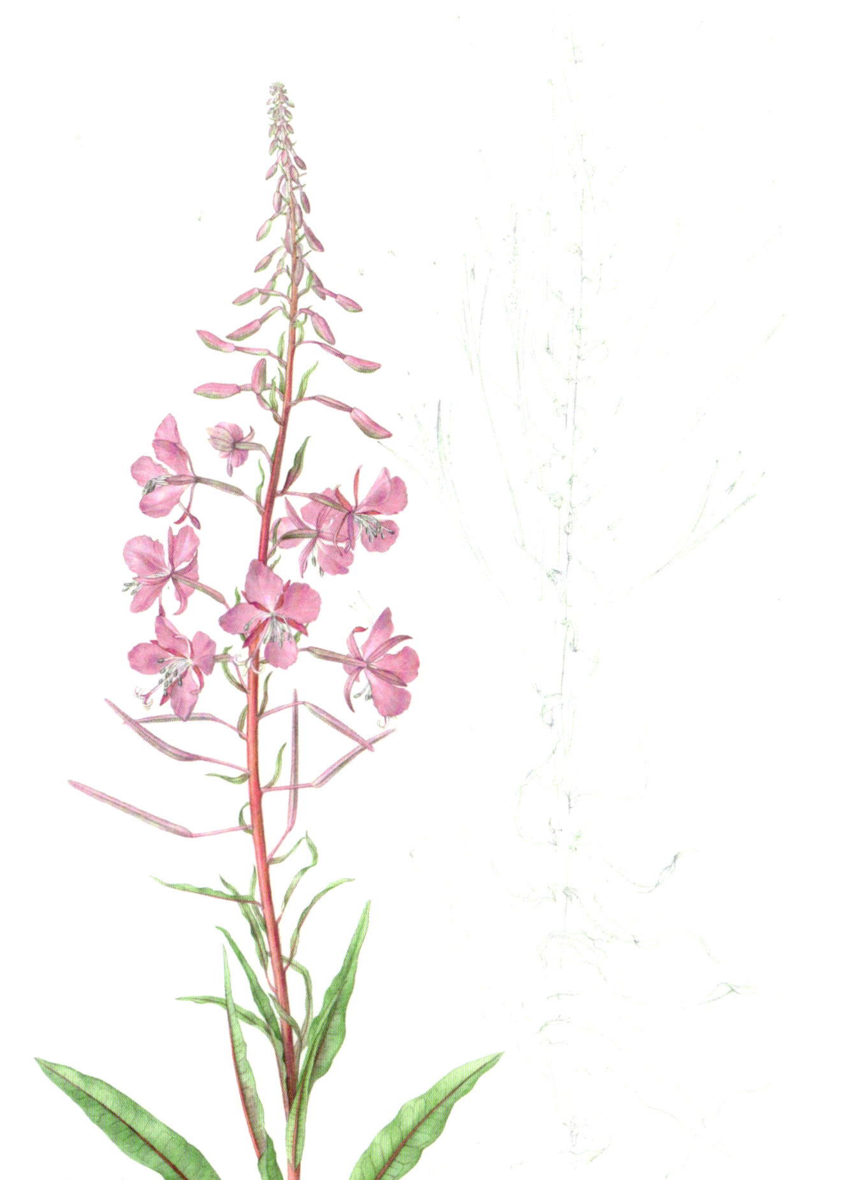

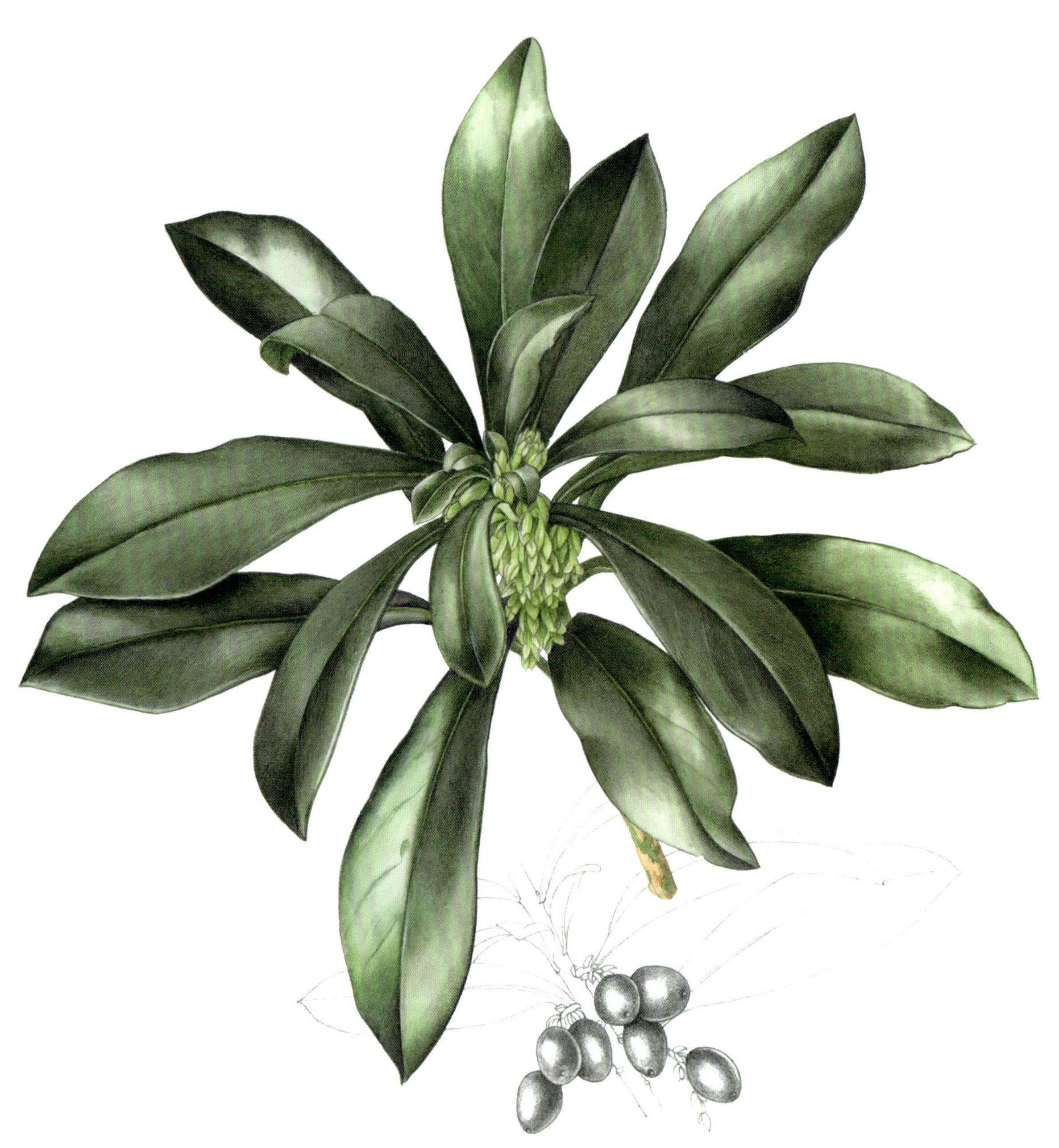

A clump of primroses,
from *A Wild Plant Year*, 2016

Opposite page:
Spurge laurel *Daphne laureola*

Spurge laurel

I was first introduced to this native plant in winter, when its clusters of lime-green flowers hang beneath the shiny, dark leaves. I found another specimen near my home for the fruits. In an illustration, the glossy black berries would have to be painted, but this would have unbalanced the composition here, so I kept them in graphite.

More of the story

Isolated plants can make striking portraits and are essential in illustrations intended to assist identification. But in reality plants have dead leaves and caterpillar holes; they grow in habitats with other species around them. I enjoy showing this in my work and telling a little more of their story.

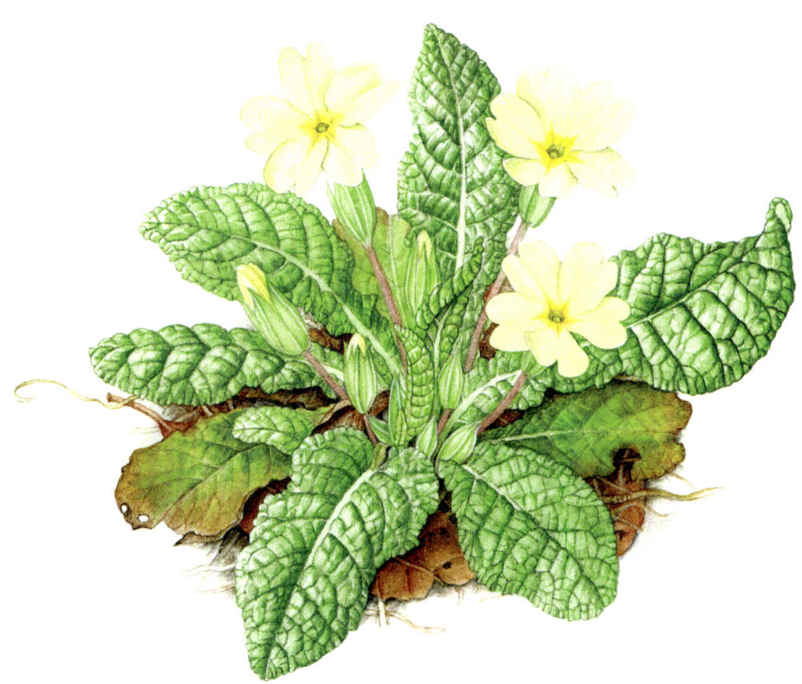

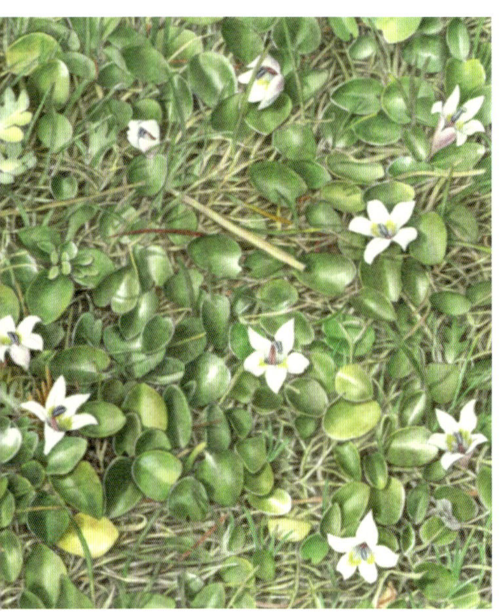

Hypsela reniformis from Cotopaxi, Ecuador, actual size

Opposite page:
Pink butterfly orchid, *Orchis* (now *Anacamptis*) *papilionacea*

Foreign natives

I have been fortunate to travel to many parts of the world to draw and paint the native flora. Plant-hunting in Europe enabled me to paint common European species that are rare in Britain, such as some orchids. More exotic destinations provided a wonderful array of species to draw and paint, as shown on the following pages. I soon learned not to carry my paintbox in my hand luggage when flying – the rectangular metal container always rang alarm bells at airport security!

South America: *Hypsela reniformis*

Halfway up the volcanic peak of Cotopaxi in Ecuador, we came across huge areas covered by this plant. I took lots of photographs and collected a few flowers and leaves to make reference drawings and notes in the relative warmth of our bus. This painting was made when I got home. I couldn't identify the plant from any of my books but some years later found it, helpfully labelled, in a Swedish botanical garden.

Wild orchids for the RHS

In the late 1980s I worked on line illustrations for *The New RHS Dictionary of Gardening* and struck up a friendship with Anthony Huxley, one of the editors. He was also on the RHS Picture Panel. Knowing his knowledge of and love for wild orchids, I took the plunge and prepared a collection of European and Australian terrestrial native orchids for the 1992 RHS London show. Sadly, Anthony died a few months before the show, so I never found out whether my paintings passed muster with him. The collection was however awarded a gold medal. It included these lovely but very variable pink butterfly orchids, drawn and photographed on the southern tip of Corsica.

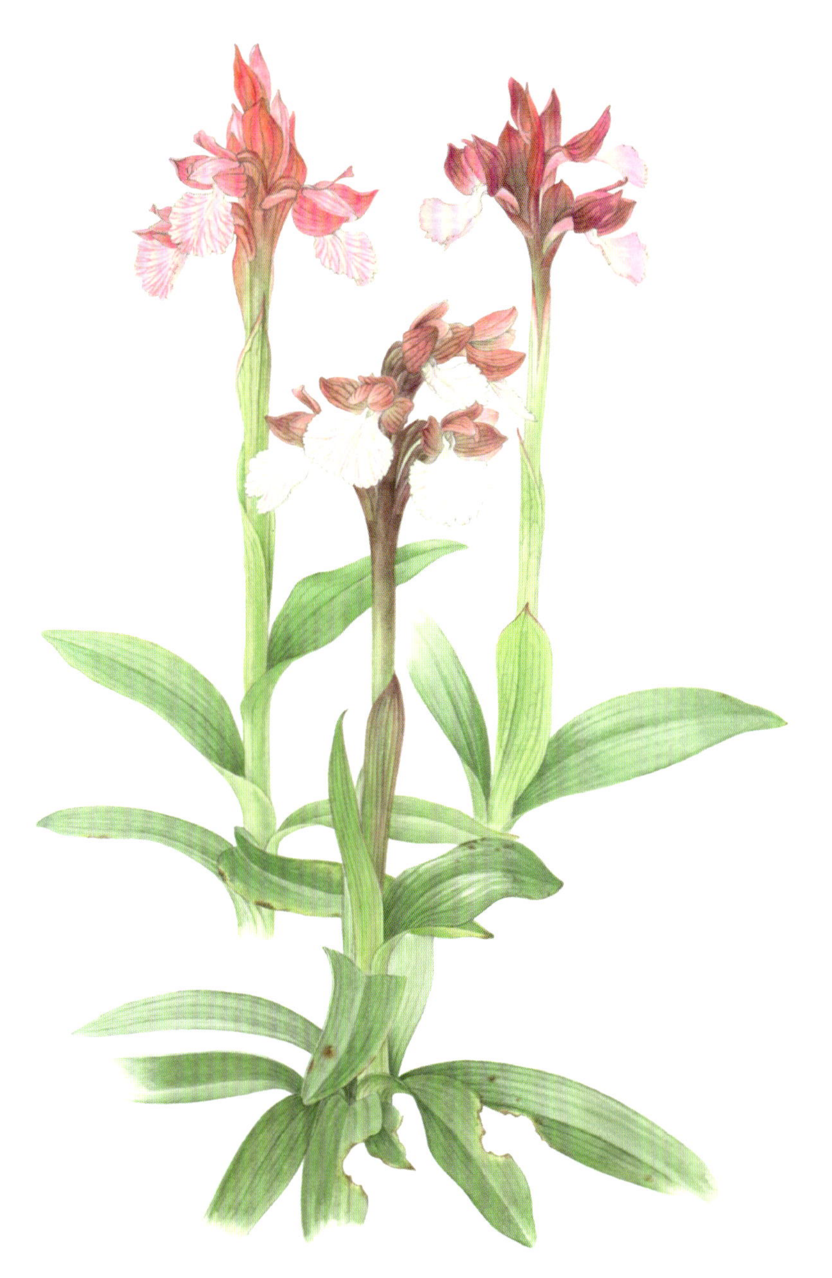

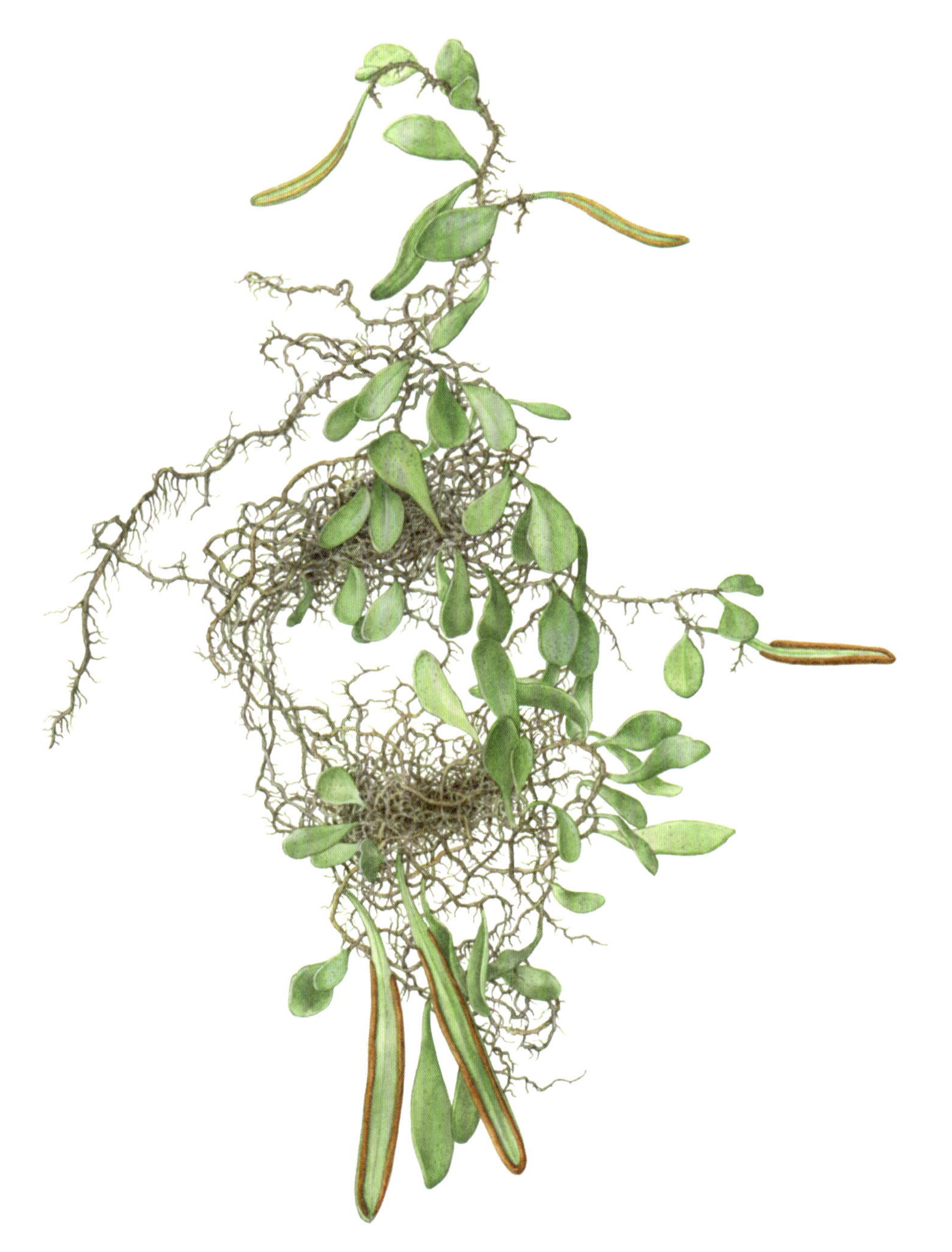

Bismarckia nobilis fruits,
Madagascar

Opposite page:
Epiphytic fern *Pyrosia pilloselloides*

Indonesia: *Pyrosia pilloselloides*

In 1993 I was the botanical illustrator to an expedition to Indonesia with wide-ranging interests, including forest canopy moths, native bees and flora. Our small group even included a conceptual artist. I worked with the botanist, collecting specimens in the rainforest and then feverishly making reference drawings and colour notes before the plants were pressed in triplicate for herbaria at Bogor (Indonesia), Harvard and Kew.

While in Jakarta, waiting for our travel permits to Sumatra, we visited the botanic gardens at Bogor and found this epiphytic fern fallen from its tree. I painted it from life in two days, working on the verandah of our bungalow where the light was good but the air-conditioning didn't reach. I had to work with a cloth held under my chin to prevent my sweat dripping onto the paper. The painting was shown in an exhibition at Kew Gardens in 1994, where one of the botanists was able to name it for me.

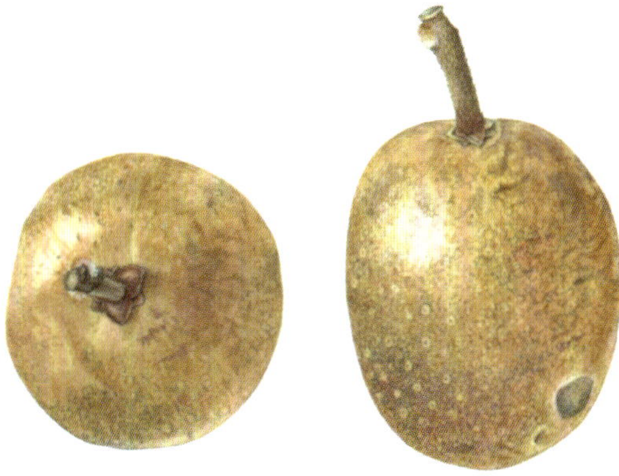

Garden plants

All our garden plants originate from native species growing somewhere in the world, though they may have been intensively bred to favour particular characteristics. Much of my illustration work has featured garden hybrids, but my personal preference is always for the simpler varieties that are closer to the wild species.

Rosa 'Climbing Cécile Brunner'

This rose thrives in my garden, climbing to the top of a tall holly tree every year. Another common name is the sweetheart rose and its pretty little chocolate-box buds are irresistible. It has a lovely perfume too.

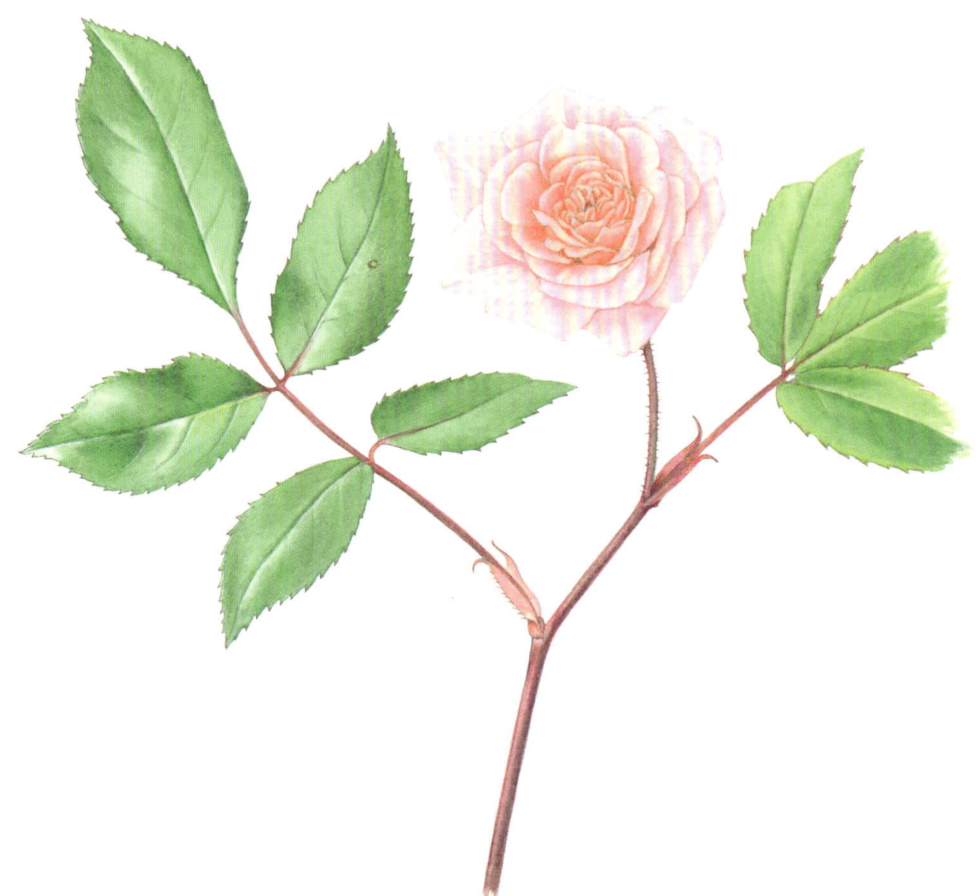

Winter treasures

These attractive fragments were picked up while walking round the Hillier Gardens in Hampshire one winter day. I never go anywhere without a bag or box in which to pop such treasures. Even in winter there are always interesting things to paint: dead leaves, fallen fruits or nuts, fragments of bark, interesting bits of twig. They do have the advantage that they won't wilt.

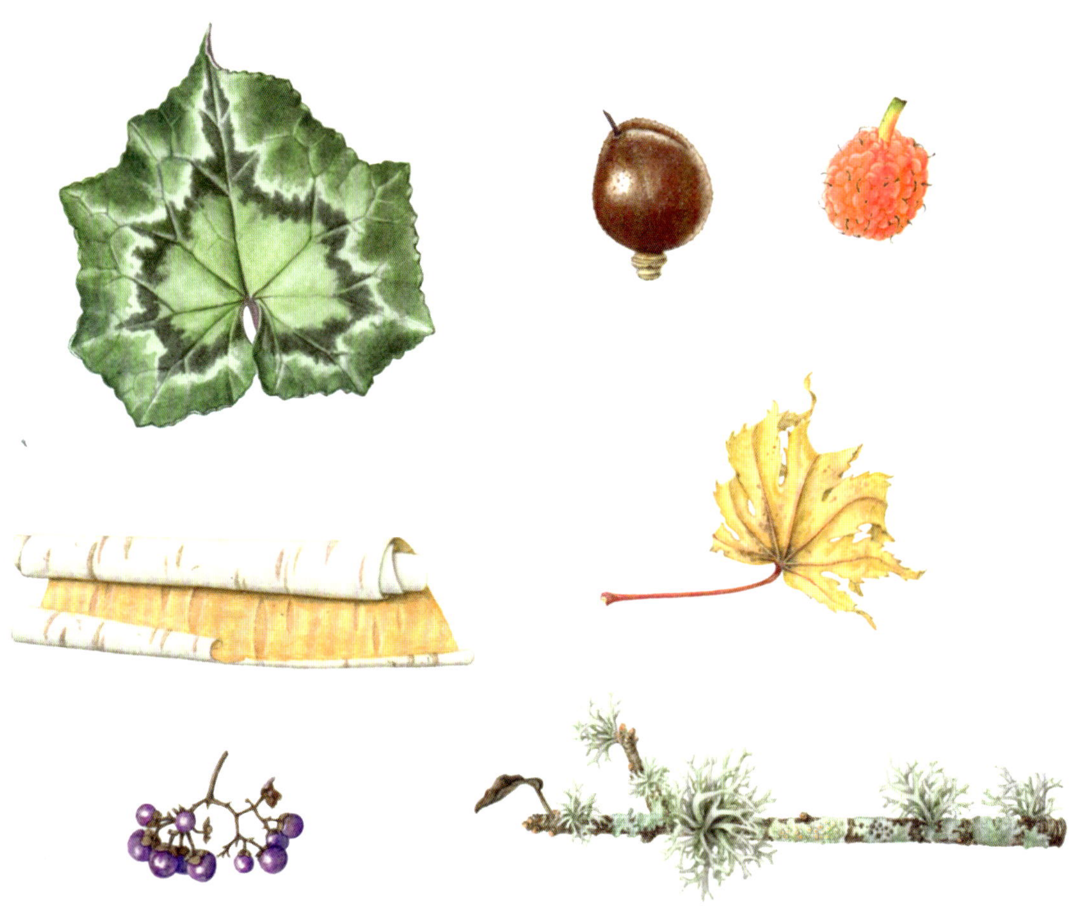

Collins Flower Guide

My biggest illustration job by far involved four years of total immersion in British flora. In 1992, Collins embarked on a wild flower guide that would cover over 1900 species and include grasses, sedges, rushes, ferns and clubmosses. The brief was to make illustrations that were scientifically accurate, made from life whenever possible, showed different stages where required, were arranged harmoniously on the page and beautiful in themselves. Not much to ask! Four artists were to share the project, but for the first six months I was working alone, making reference paintings of plants in my chosen families. The following pages show how I made illustrations from these resources.

Having to paint unfamiliar subjects was a good way to learn how they work, and how to recognise their relatives. I had to source my own subjects, which I collected from my local habitats, observing the laws on collecting wild plants (see note on page 66) and only taking the minimum needed. The rare plants I drew and photographed in situ as best I could. I also had a great deal of help from field naturalists far and wide; two kind gentlemen – who I exchanged emails with but never met – sent me sprigs of all the willows whose only British sites were in the Scottish highlands.

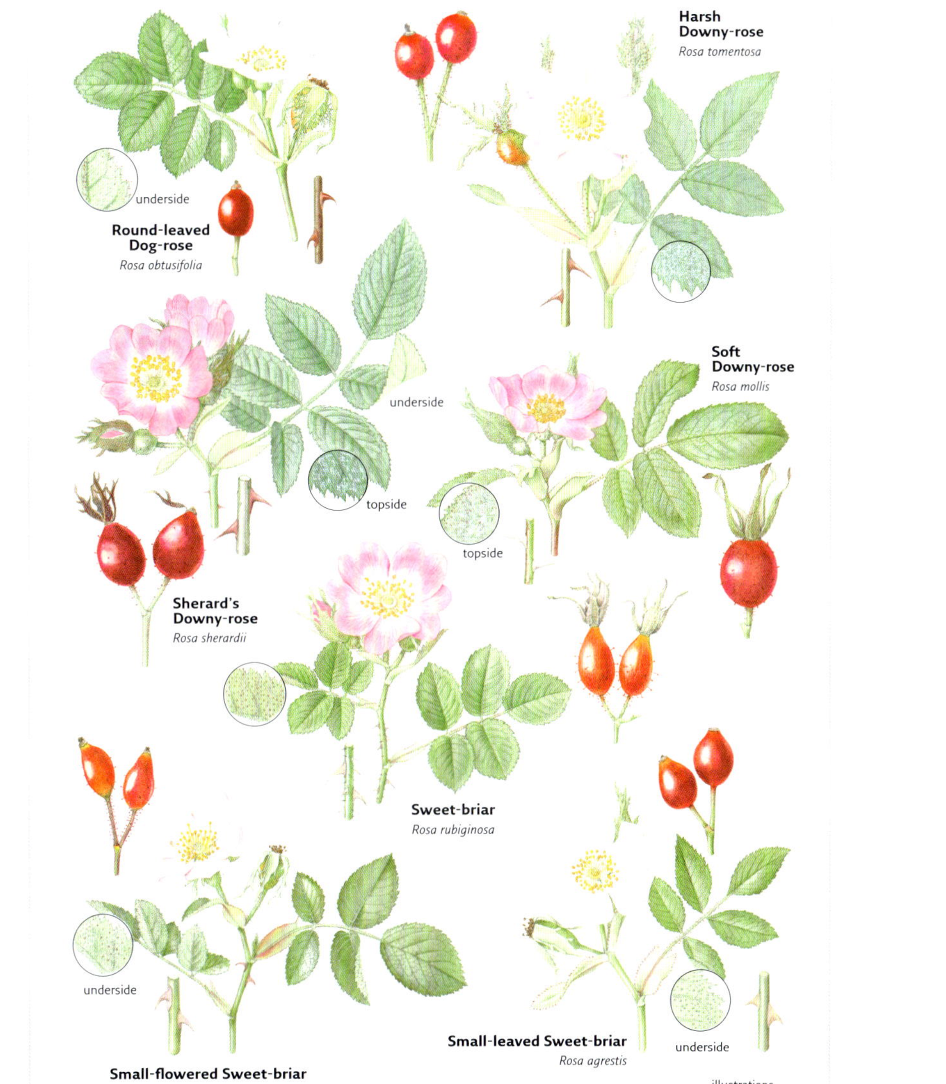

Harsh
Downy-rose
Rosa tomentosa

Round-leaved
Dog-rose
Rosa obtusifolia

underside

Soft
Downy-rose
Rosa mollis

underside

topside

topside

Sherard's
Downy-rose
Rosa sherardii

Sweet-briar
Rosa rubiginosa

Small-flowered Sweet-briar
Rosa micrantha

underside

Small-leaved Sweet-briar
Rosa agrestis

underside

illustrations
0.6× lifesize

Normally I work with the plant subject in front of me, but the Collins guide required eight species per plate on average. The likelihood of having all eight to hand at once – and of keeping them alive until the pencil roughs were approved – was close to zero. So I made reference drawings from life, took photographs and pressed specimens; I made life-size sketches from different angles and at different stages; and I also made lots of notes, including colour notes. There is never enough time to complete a painting in the field, and colours on photographs can't always be trusted, so colour notes are vital.

Over the years I have amassed a library of such reference material. I never throw it away – some illustrations in the Collins guide were painted from sketches made twenty years earlier.

Having checked with the author exactly which features are required, I gather together all my references. The plants are drawn at life size, composed in a rectangle that can be reduced to the required size. This first rough drawing has many arrows and notes indicating adjustments to the composition.

Next, the rough is reduced to A4 and traced onto the painting paper using a light box and a fine 3H pencil. I take account of the necessary adjustments and constantly refer back to my original sketches. This final pencil rough is then scanned and sent to the author for approval or correction.

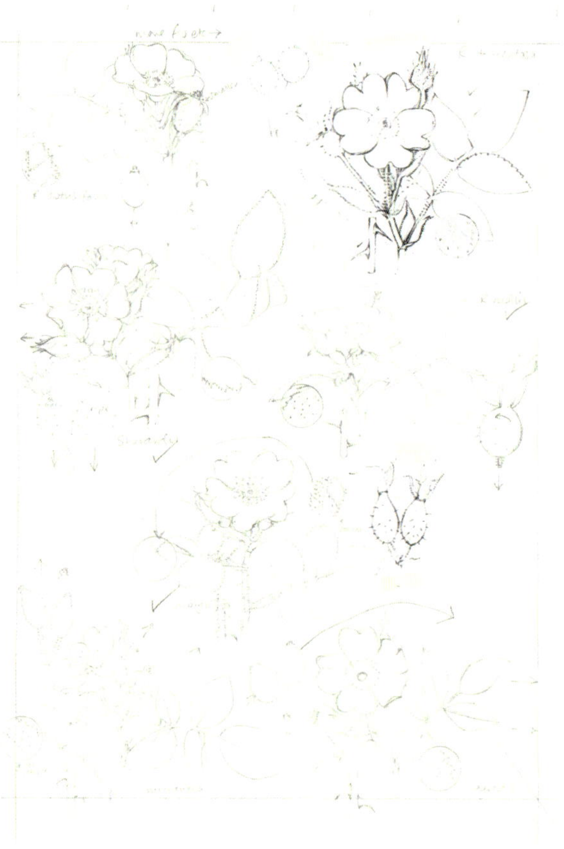

Once the final rough is approved, I paint it, once again referring back to the original sketches. The challenge is to go through all these mechanical processes and still achieve lifelike results.

R micrantha

? micrantha
cross?

smaller flo,
paler, white
centre, greyish
veins

lemon disk +
anthers

in young flo anthers fat
+ cadmium filaments
disk ditto, styles p gr

1 unripe

NB Dandy says to ind/for
w reflexed sepals as
in Rose Handbook

size x

glands on
calyx lvs
refl on top
hairs so
much

branches

same col as lf

backs
lighter, mat
veins yellower,
quite thick + proud

CHECK shd be glands
all over backs, or
just on veins + edges

tips
quite
lumpy

glands
red
buds ie as it's
fallen bracts

dk w hair veins
glands all round

lv veins
n white lf

lvs yellower
than R canina
more sheen —
dk + th lf
lvr veins

red br glands

Acc to C.G.W descrip,
lvs shd be rounded at base,
cf R agrestis, where narrowed

lvs sheen
w glossy
hairless
glandular
edge cups

glands
red edge

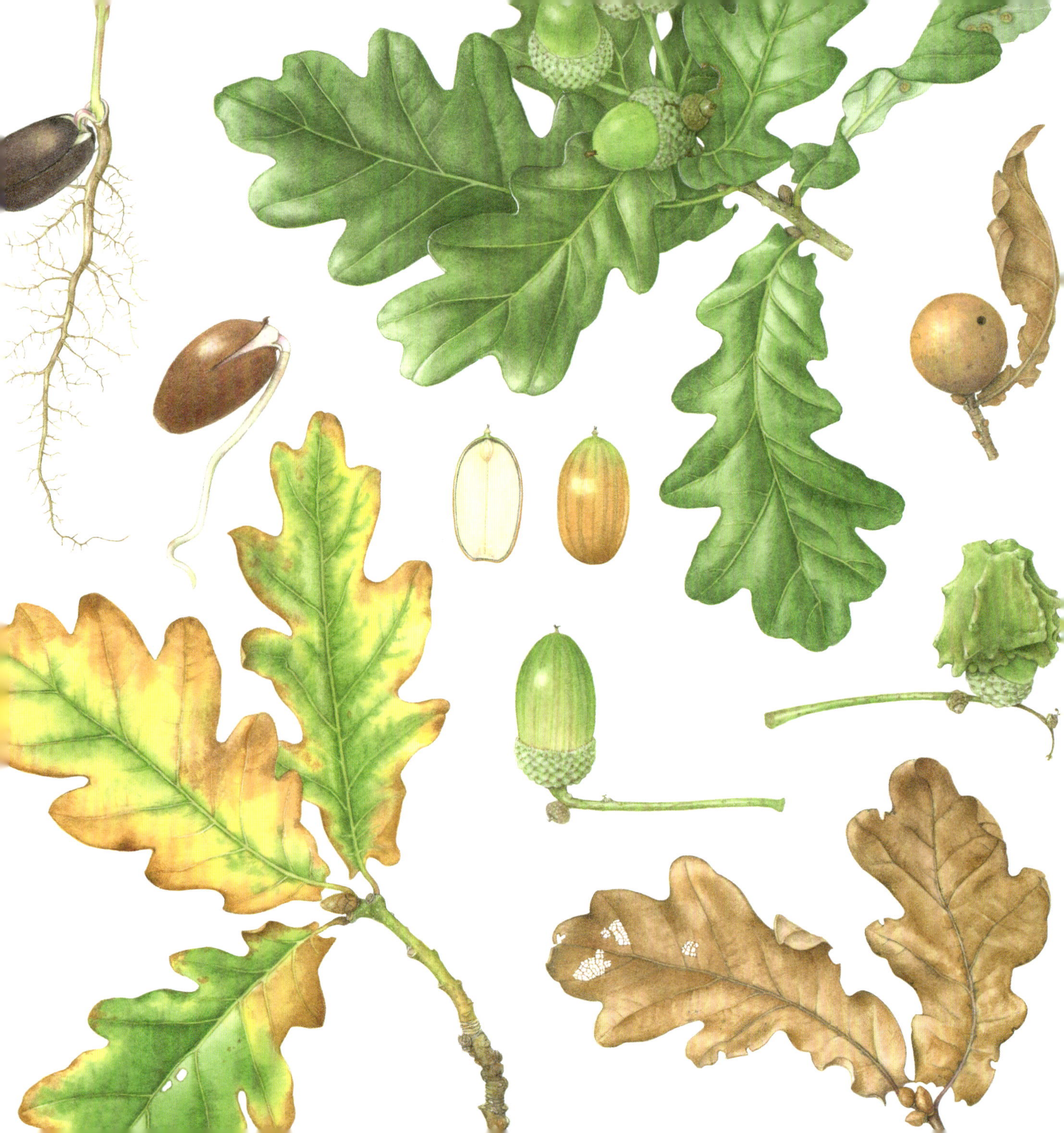

Life stories, and the relatives

Life stories, and the relatives

From seedling to decay

An illustrator is often required to show different stages in the life cycle of a plant, though rarely the seedling or the skeleton leaf. However, all the stages of a plant's growth fascinate me, and they are favoured subjects for my exhibition work, although compositions that are added to over time do require some planning. The Inside Story on page 32 explains my process.

Cyclamen cycle

I love *Cyclamen hederifolium* in autumn and winter. The delicate flowers are a delight, and the patterned leaves are a painting challenge, involving some lifting and a lot of dry brush work. I really enjoy the madly spiralling stems of the developing fruits.

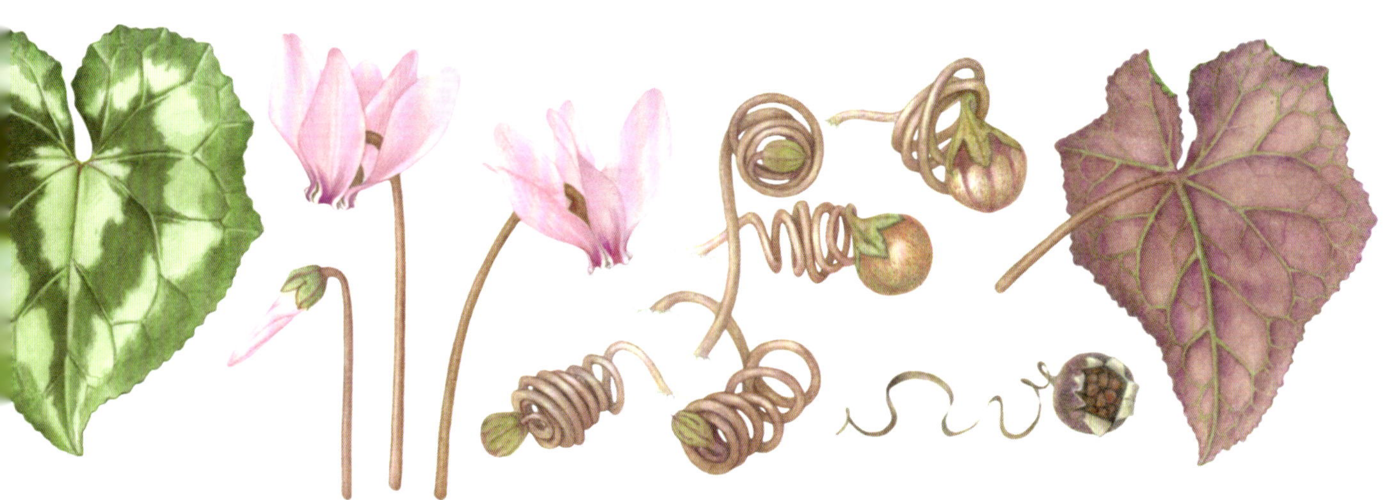

Snowdrop shoots

Finding winter depressingly cold and dark, I am always cheered by the first snowdrop shoots emerging from last year's leaf litter. When painting them, I work from snowdrops I have potted up, and from dead leaves collected in autumn. This image was made for *A Wild Plant Year* to illustrate the festivals of Candlemas and Imbolc, which both celebrate the increasing light at the beginning of February.

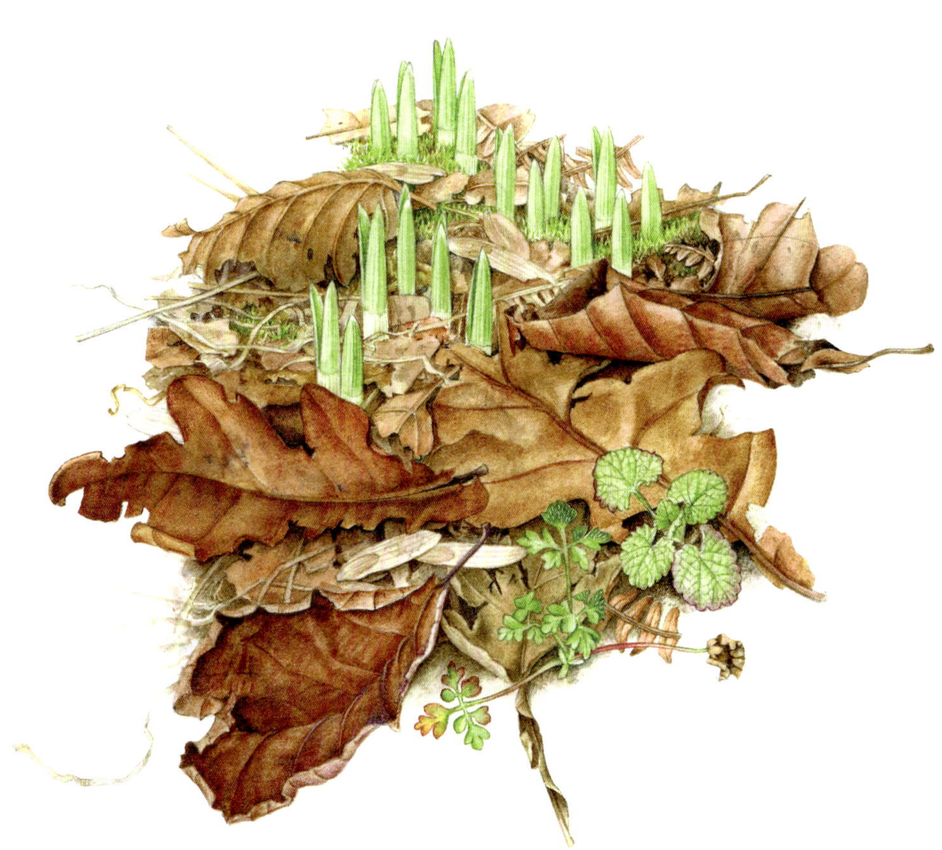

Skeleton crew

Opposite page:
English oak *Quercus robur*

Skeleton crew
At the other end of their life cycle, some plants are reduced to their bare bones, as it were. These skeletons show the structures that once gave strength or carried nutrients around the plants. One can learn a lot of botany by looking at skeletons. I paint them with a very dry brush.

English, common, or pedunculate oak
This painting took over a year to complete, as the different elements became available in the course of the seasons. It was one in a series of similar paintings of British native trees that I made while working on my book *The Greenwood Trees*. They were designed as exhibition pieces, but some parts were used as illustrations for that book.

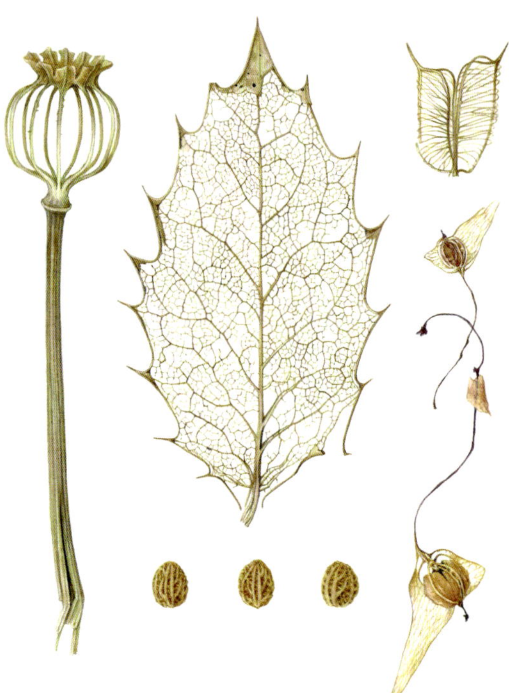

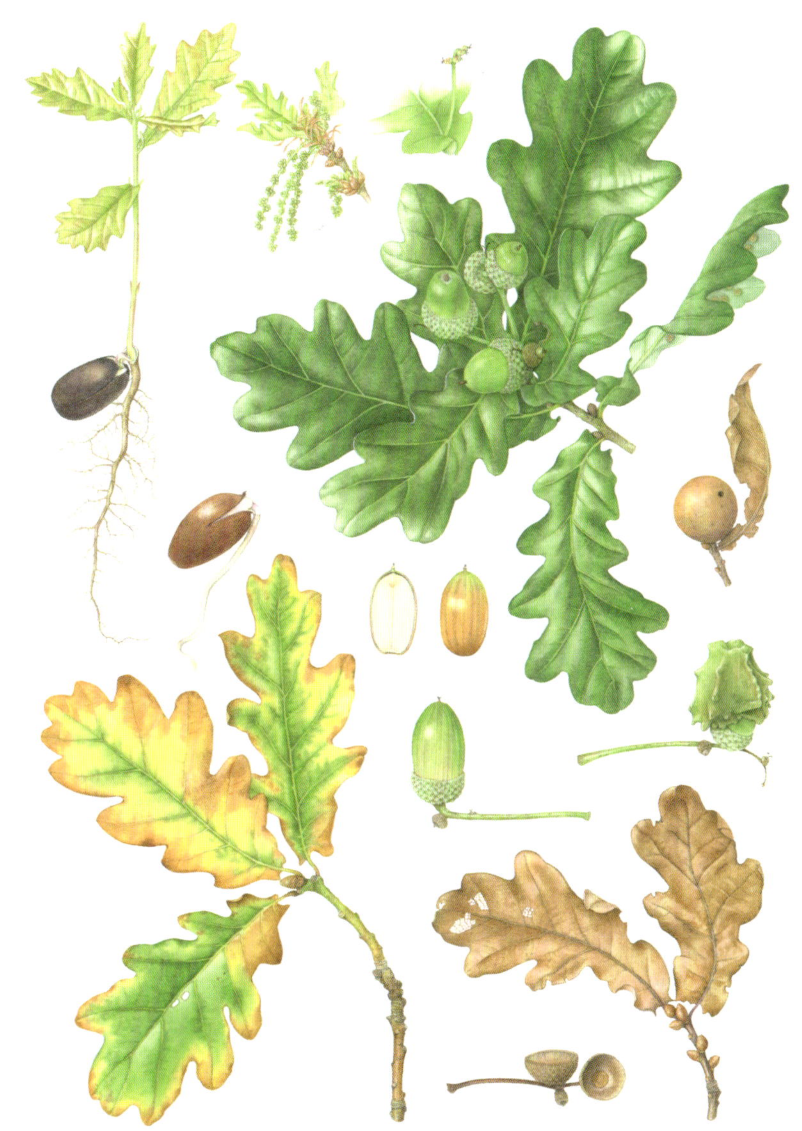

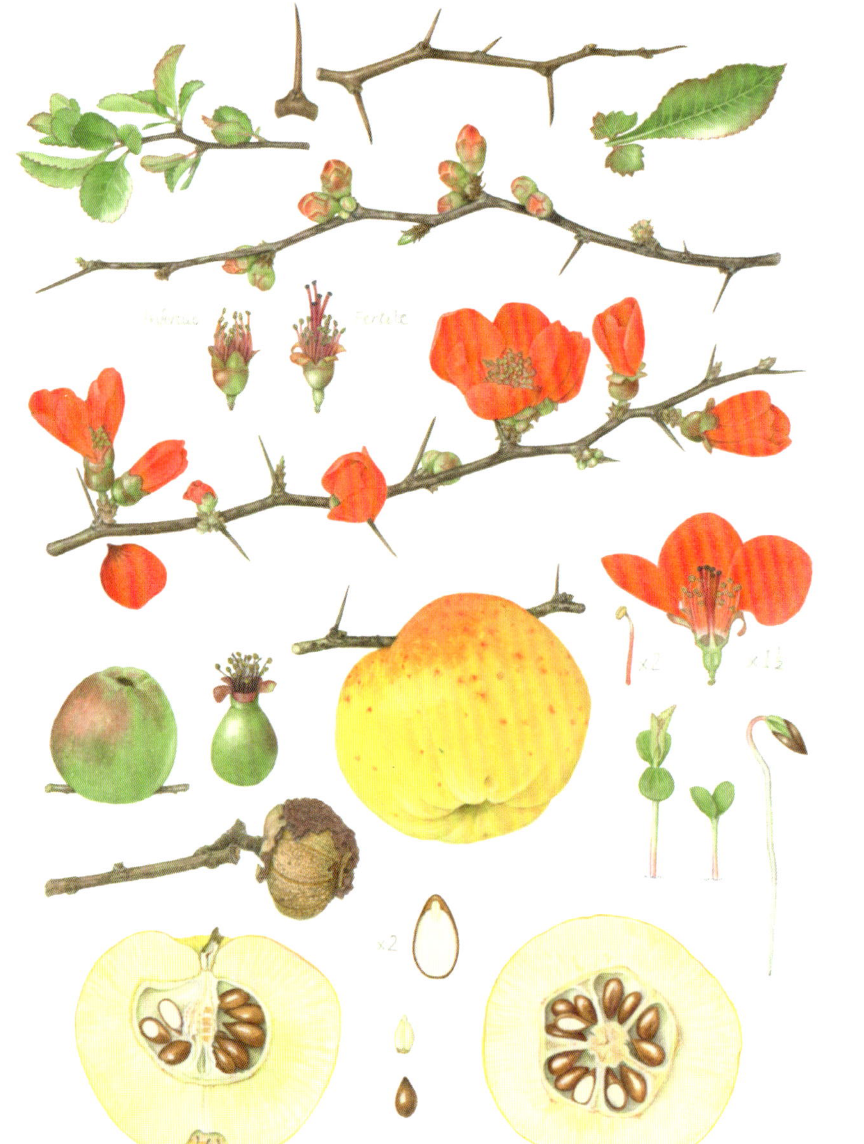

Fruits of plants in the *Fabaceae* (pea family)

Opposite page:
Japanese quince *Chaenomeles speciosa* hybrid

Japanese quince

The jewel-bright blossom of this plant so early in the year is heartening, and I love the bright yellow fruits in autumn and winter too. I have several times painted the whole life cycle in one image. This particular painting proved rather problematic though. The composition wasn't working, so I added extra bits to fill gaps, which made other gaps apparent. I ended up searching desperately for more elements to balance it all – even last year's wizened, mummified fruits.

The relatives

When travelling in other countries, I often half-recognise a plant. It may remind me of a plant I know but isn't quite 'right'. Frequently, it turns out to be in the same family as the plant I know. Making paintings that show several related plants in a kind of 'compare and contrast' exercise has become an enjoyable challenge for me: the detective-work is great fun.

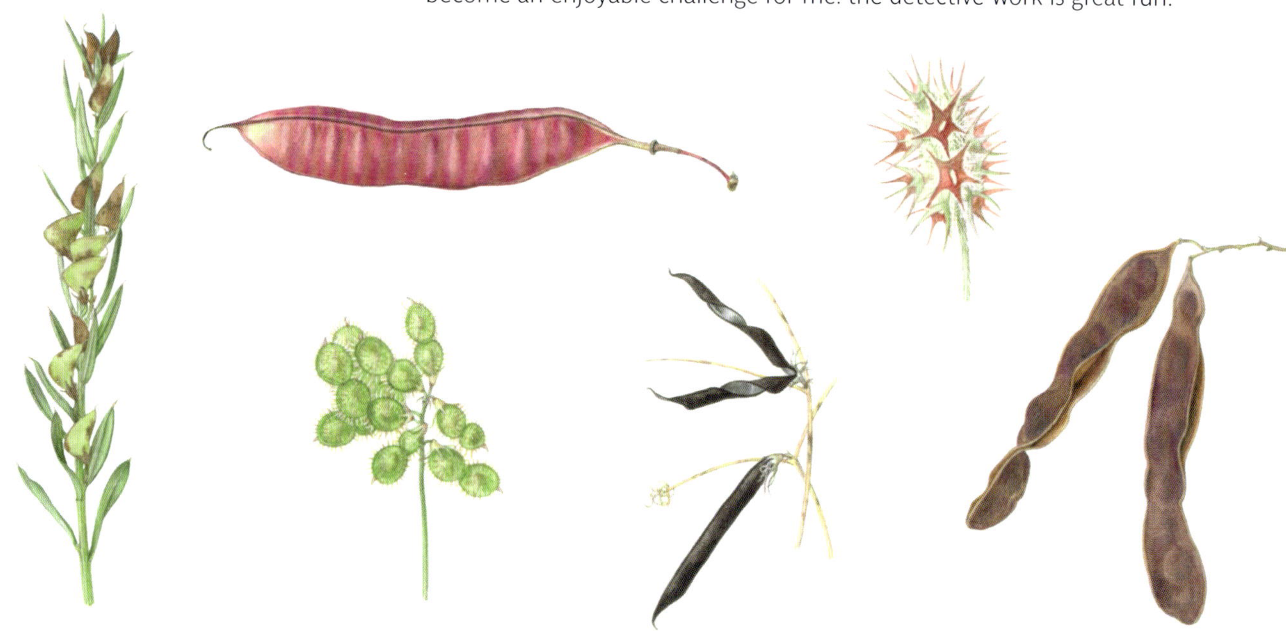

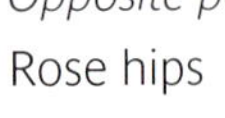

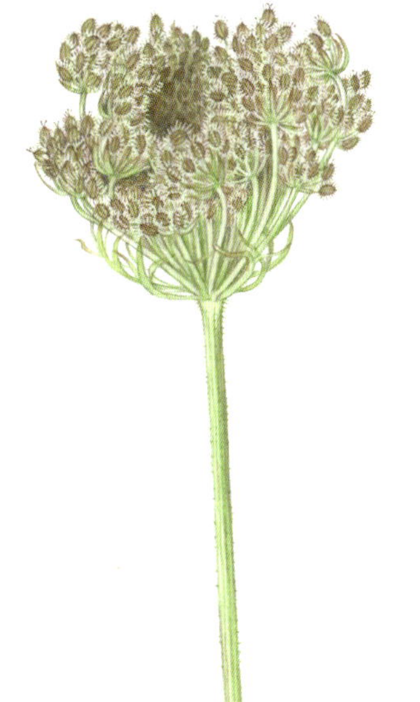

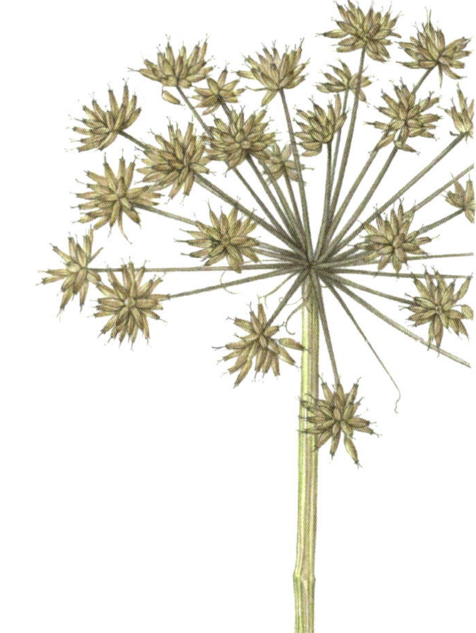

Umbellifer fruits

The Umbellifer family (now called Apiaceae) have all their flowering stems springing – umbrella-style – from a single point on the main stem. (One of my students once aptly misnamed them 'umbrellifers'.) Studying the seeds can help to identify the various species within the family. The three shown here all grow wild in Britain.

Rose hips

Wanting to make a colourful painting without too much white space, I started a picture with some big, fat rose hips left over from a workshop. I chose a square format because I had a spare mount and it is a useful shape for greetings cards. As the painting progressed, I found myself searching for rose hips to fit the remaining spaces perfectly. It was tempting to bend a few stems to the required angle! I took scans and kept a diary to explain my composition process. These notes and images make up the Inside Story on composition that follows.

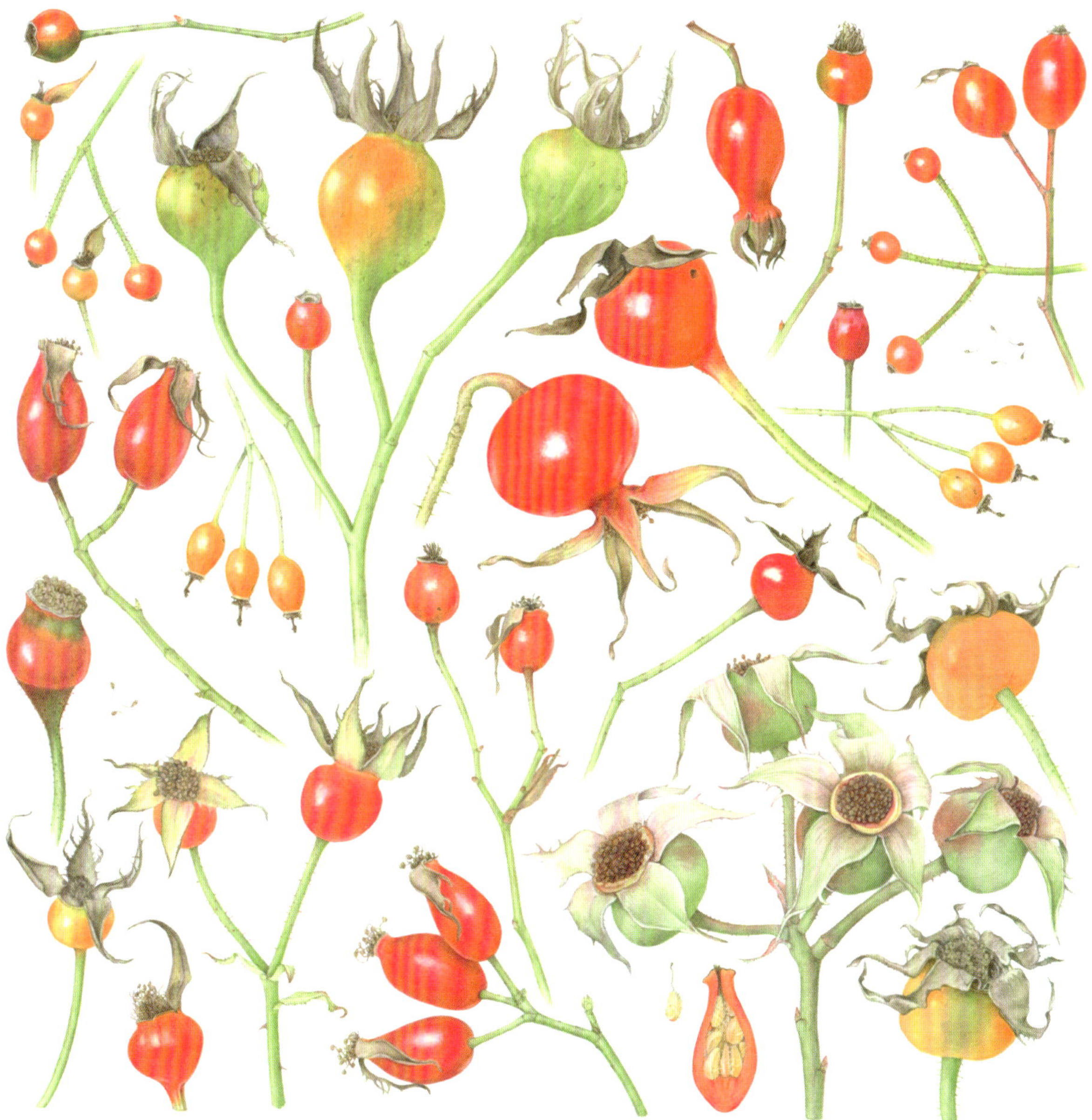

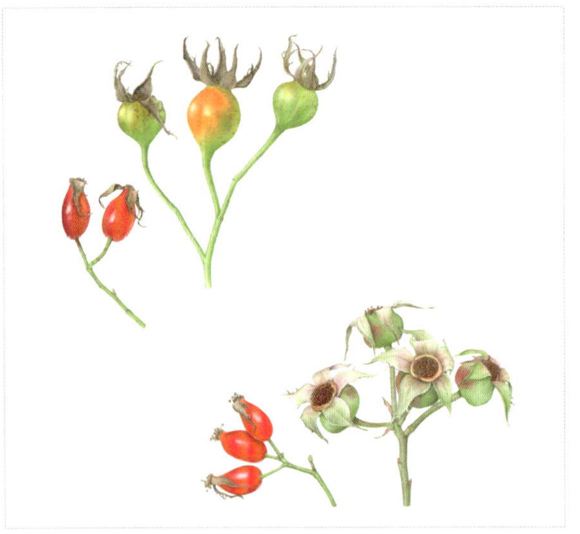

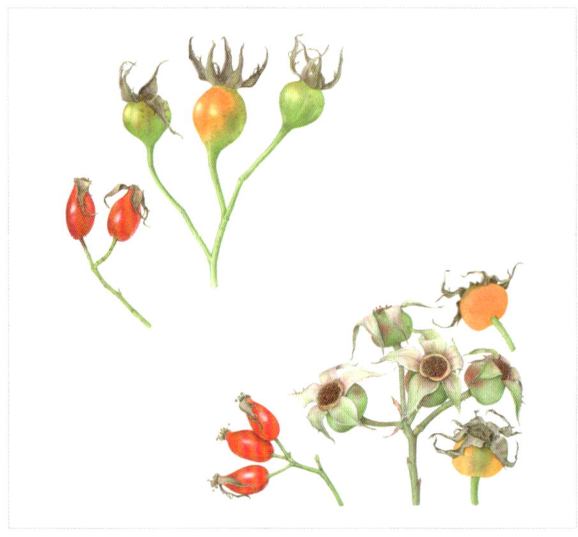

Stage 1

Will probably want a *Rosa rugosa* hip, maybe two, and that will be a very heavy compositional element, so will leave space fairly centrally.

Stage 2

Some new peach-coloured hips go opposite the orange-blushed ones at the top. Don't want too much orange but do need another splash in the bottom left, for balance. Think some small, pendent or even upside-down hips will fill in gaps, but need bigger red ones in place first. Also considering a dissection, possibly falling sepals.

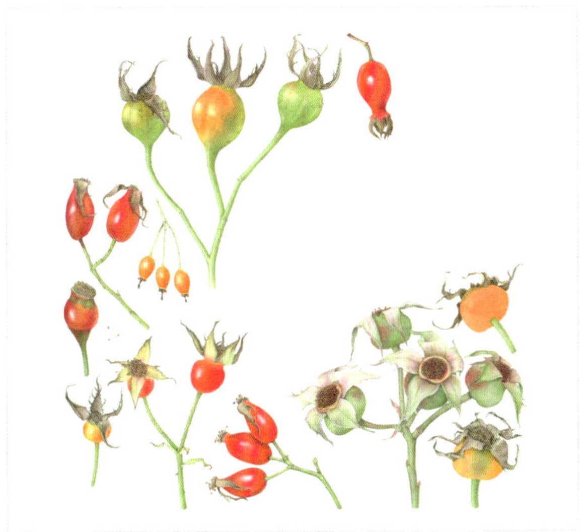 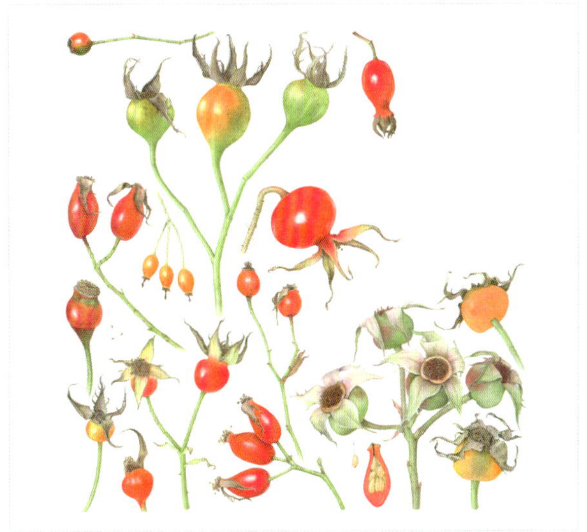

Stage 3

Now have some lovely small pendent hips and a glorious *R moyesii* flask. Have decided to make a 'river' of red hips in a rough diagonal bottom left to top right. Finding hips to fit spaces is increasingly challenging. Using tracing paper to sketch hips and place them carefully. Wondering whether to include lettering to help fill spaces.

Stage 4

Have been given more hips, including a *Rosa rugosa*, and some very useful tiny ones. Composition looks rather 'bitty' – extending some of the cut stems might help. Then think of fading the ends out instead, so use the lifting brush, and it does look much better. The eye subconsciously extends the stems further.

Think the horizontal specimen at the top was a mistake but there is nothing to be done about it, so will put more horizontal stems in to balance it. Lots of sympathetic rhythms (stems at the same or almost the same angle) building up, so will look for opportunities to include more. Great temptation to fill every space but finally call a halt. Amazing how much better the composition looks when mounted – benefit of using a mount frequently during the painting process.

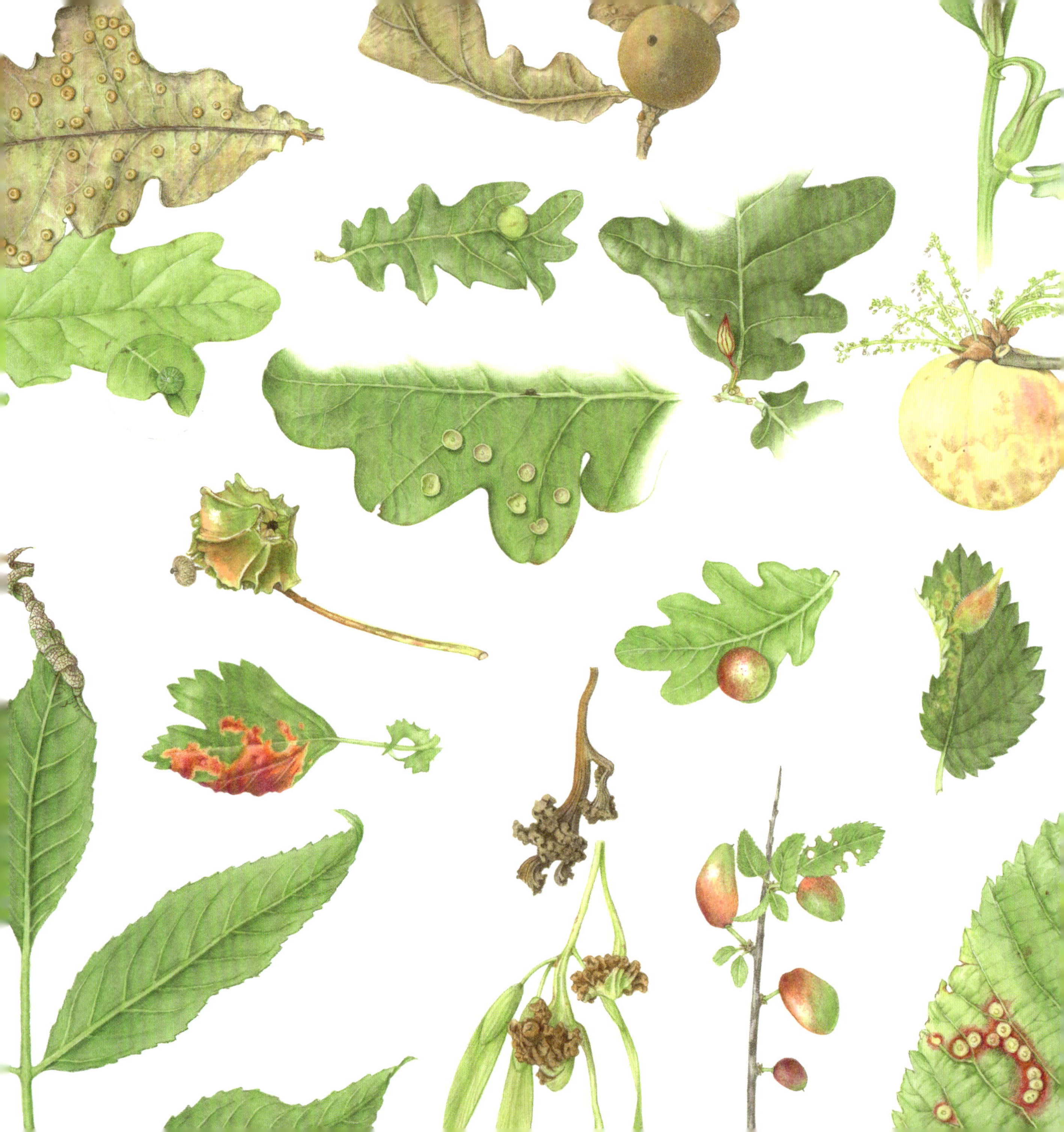

Section 3
The supporting cast

Jay feathers

A blue tit's nest, found abandoned with eggs in, painted for *The Greenwood Trees*, 2018

Opposite page:
Peacock butterfly on buddleia, painted for a Wildlife Trust project on pollinators

Previous page:
Galls on native trees

The supporting cast

Invertebrates, birds and other animals are often interdependent with plants, so they, too, have a part in the whole story. My illustration work has included several books and projects that featured insects or other animals, and once even slugs. Butterflies, beetles and moths, too, appear in my exhibition paintings on occasion, and not always to cover an accidental paint spot! I try to make these creatures as naturalistic as possible, so I study how they move, fly, feed and settle. Even if the animals themselves do not appear, I like to include evidence of their activity, such as caterpillar holes in leaves, empty eggshells or fallen feathers.

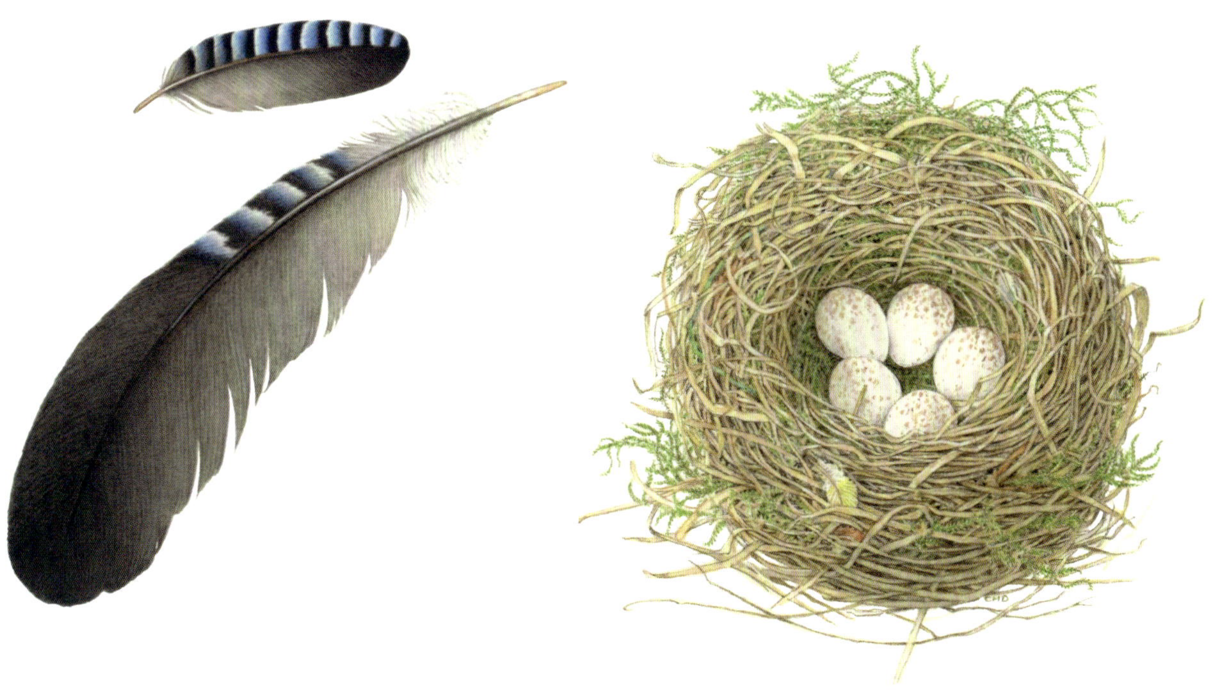

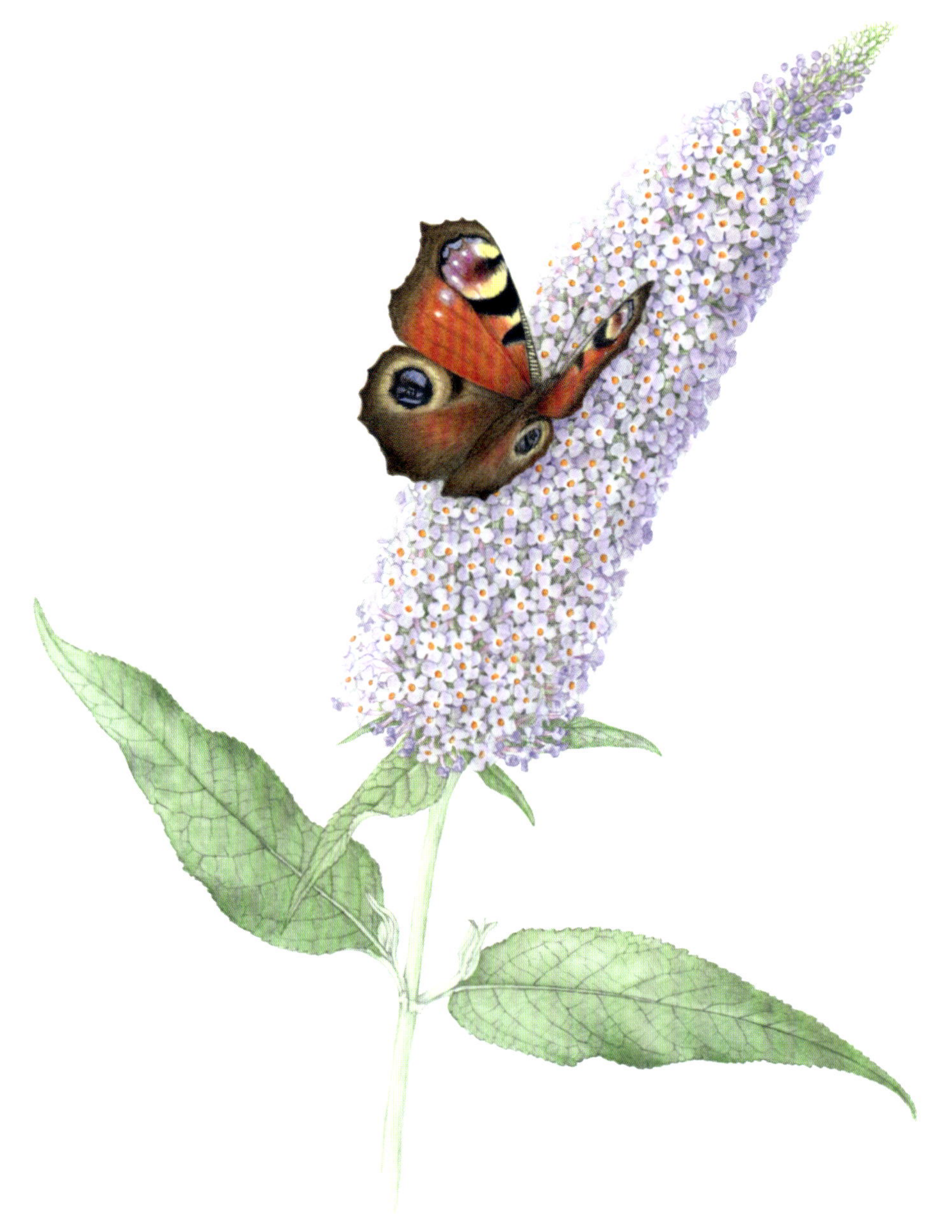

SIGNS

Pine cone gnawed by grey squirrel
Hazelnuts
1. young squirrel
2 adult
1
2
Oak marble gall of Andricus kollari
Upturned clumps of moss left by blackbirds hunting for grubs
Snail shell broken on stone 'anvil' by thrush
Blackbird egg shell
Cast snake skin
Dropping of seed-eating bird
Caddisfly larva case
Barn owl pellet
Rabbit droppings
Hazels eaten by wood mice
Jay feather
Damselfly nymph case
Leafcutter bee damage
Christina Hart-Davies

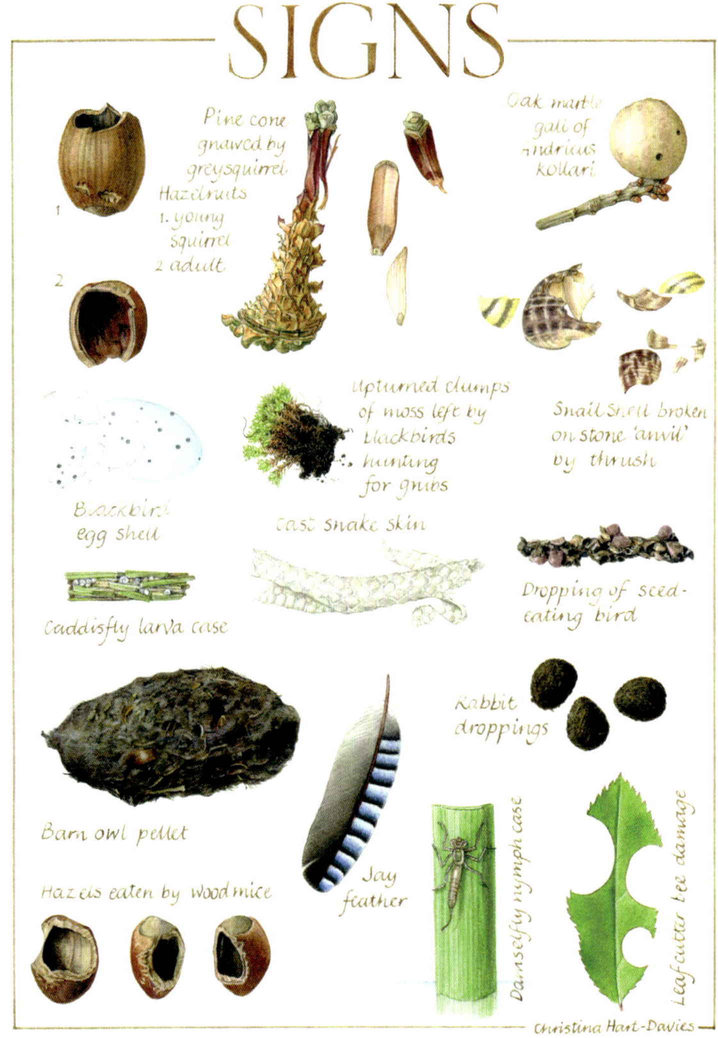

Signs

This painting was made for a joint exhibition on the wild plants and animals found in the famous Sir Harold Hillier Gardens in Hampshire. Visitors come to see the trees and cultivated plants, but there is a wealth of native flora and fauna there too. My artist colleagues specialised in painting the fauna, so I made this composition of the signs it leaves behind. Later I made another painting of the owl pellet deconstructed: it was composed largely of beetle wing cases, fur and the tiny bones of shrews.

Six-spot burnet moths

In 2016 I was asked to visit a site near my home to check on a report of a rare plant growing there. While hunting for the plant, I was delighted to find hundreds of newly-hatched six-spot burnet moths nearby. The many reference drawings and photographs taken that day enabled me to paint moth illustrations and this mug design for a wildlife trust – see page 43 for the Inside Story on painting these moths. And yes, I found the rare plant, too!

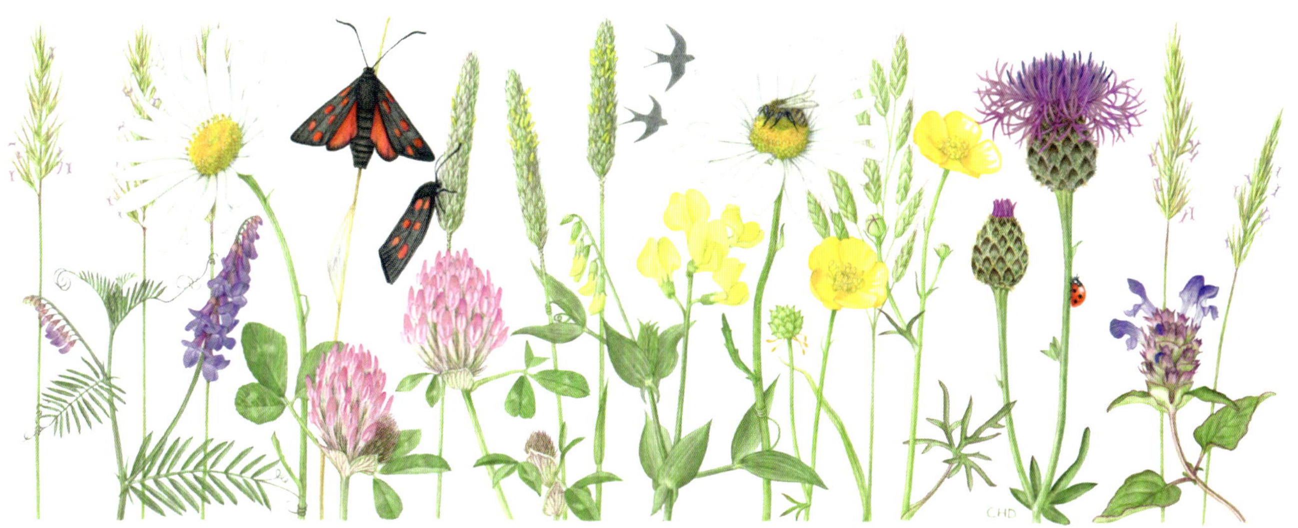

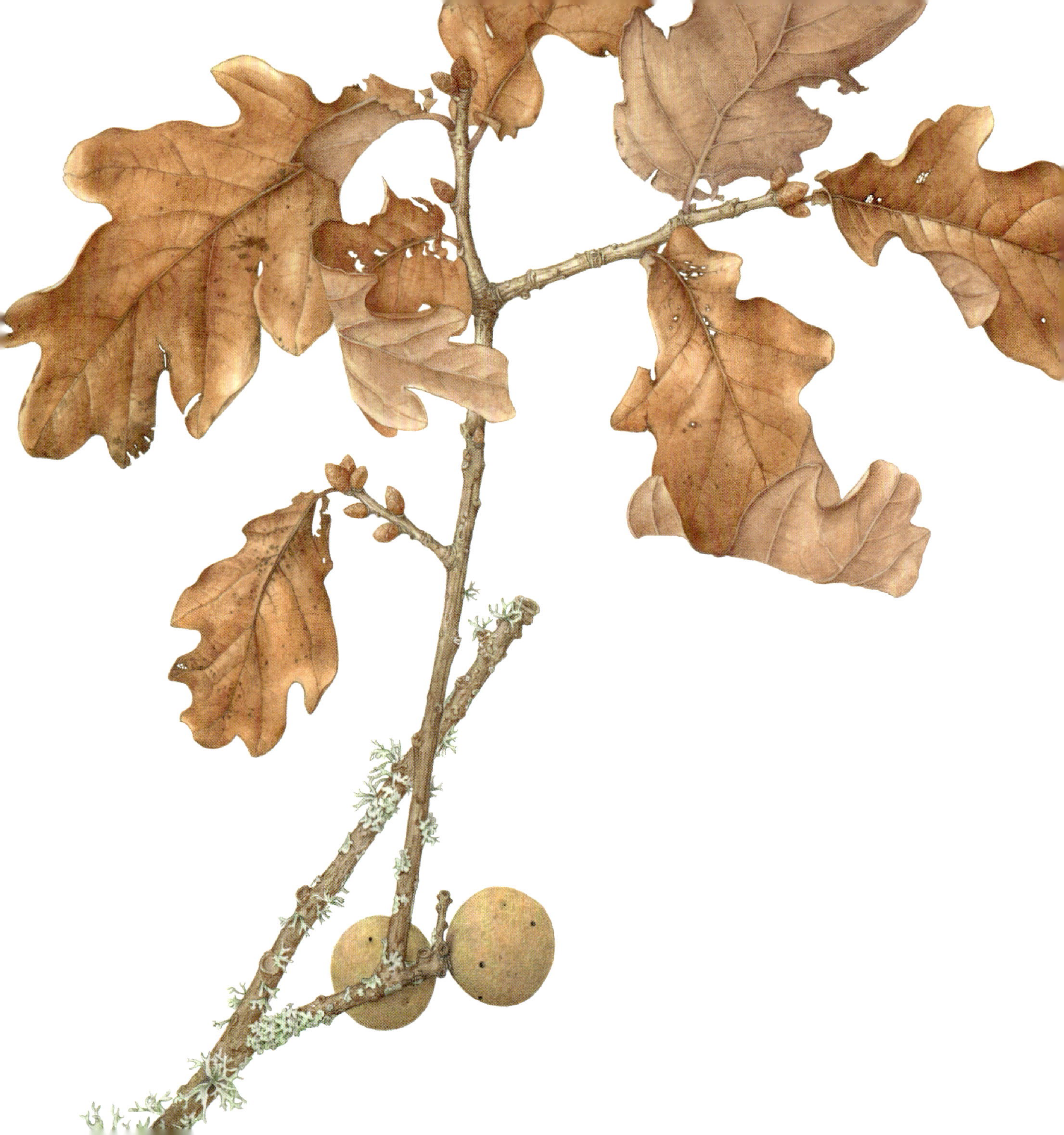

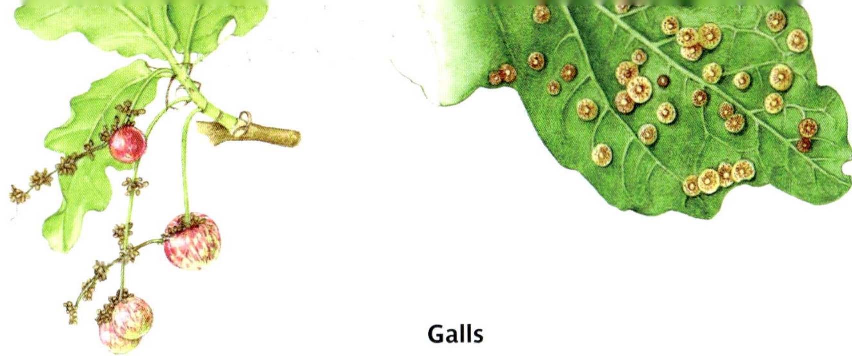

Galls

Galls fascinate me. They are abnormal growths on plants, often very oddly shaped. They are caused by the chemicals released when an insect or other invertebrate lays its egg on a plant. These disrupt the plant's hormones, stimulating it to produce the gall that will envelop the egg. When the egg hatches, the larva develops inside the gall and finally emerges as an adult. Many gall insects have a complicated life cycle involving alternating generations, each with a differently shaped gall. Gall-causing invertebrates are usually specific to a single host, but some trees are attacked by many different species. Our native common oak, *Quercus robur*, is said to host over forty of them.

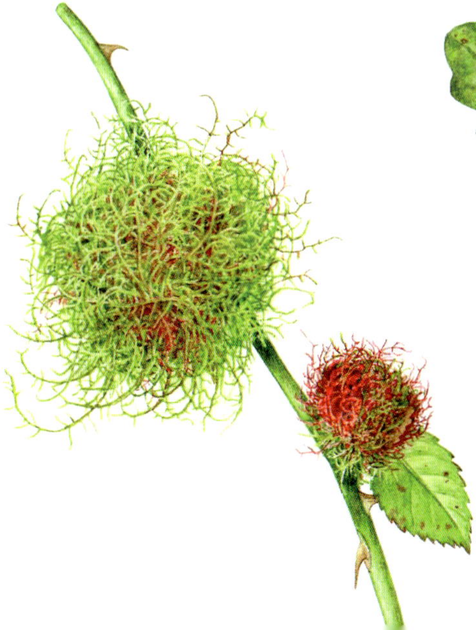

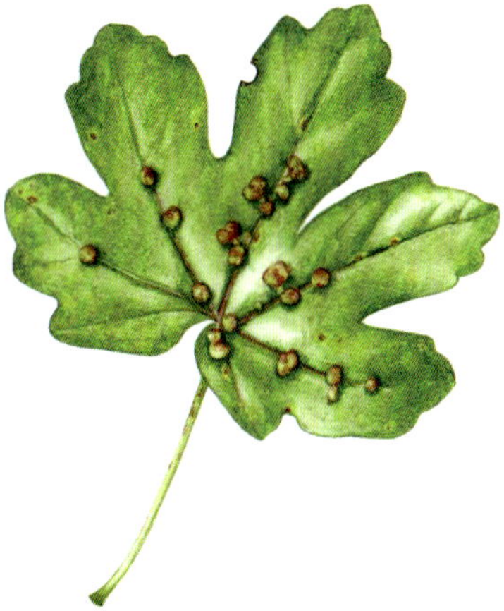

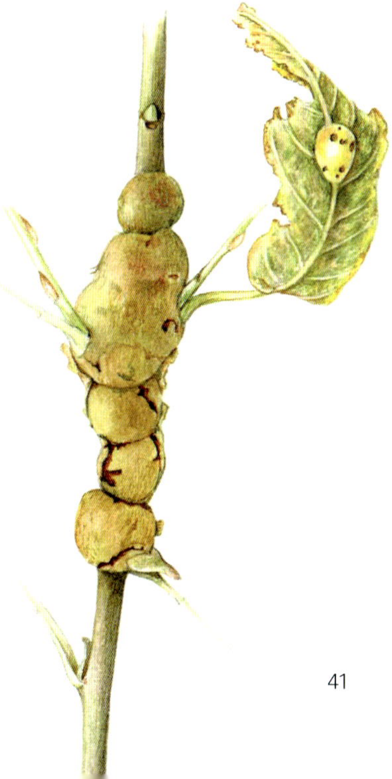

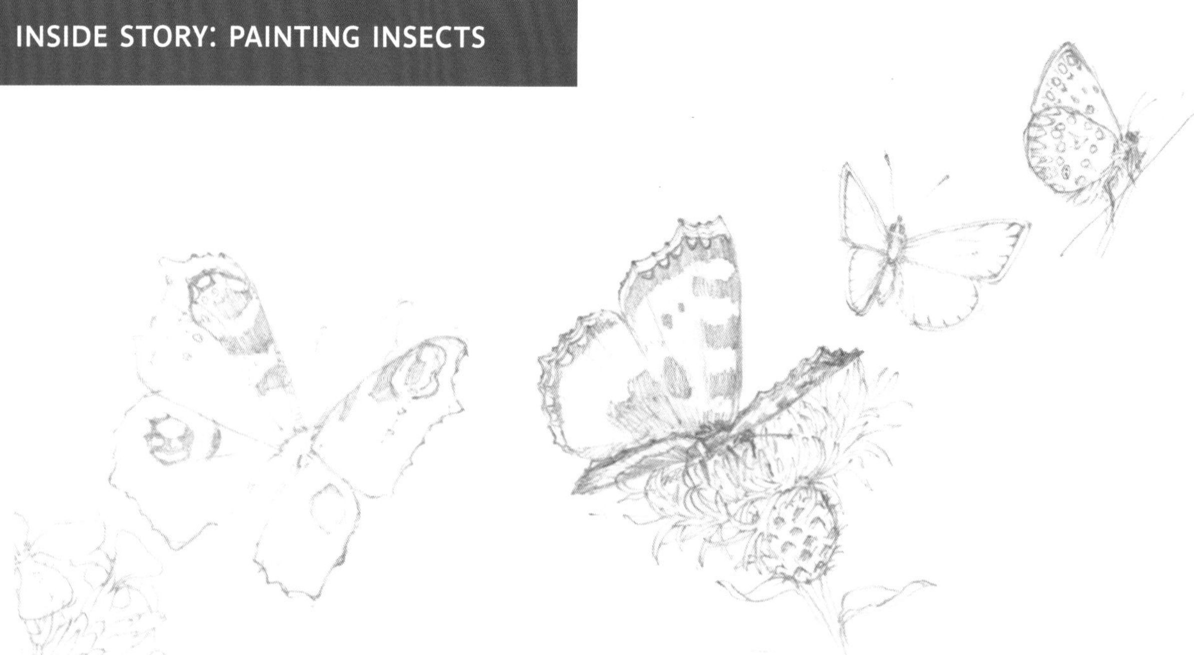

Painting insects

I have a small pinned collection of common British butterflies and also collect dead bees, moths and even odd wings, whenever I find them. After a few days in the freezer to kill any mites, they will last for several years if kept dry. Their colours fade and their pose may not be lifelike, but they are a useful reference for proportions and textures. I also watch living insects to see how they hold themselves when flying, settling and feeding, and I take lots of photographs too, to use as reference. Direct copying from other people's photographs without their permission infringes copyright law.

Drawing

Many moths settle with their wings held flat, but butterflies often do not. For insects that obligingly rest flat, I can establish a central line, draw the wings and legs on one side and then trace these on to the other side. This achieves symmetry, but I have to take care not to let the body become too broad in the process. For butterflies that don't rest with their wings flat, I draw the wings on one side from a pinned specimen and then add those on the second side in perspective.

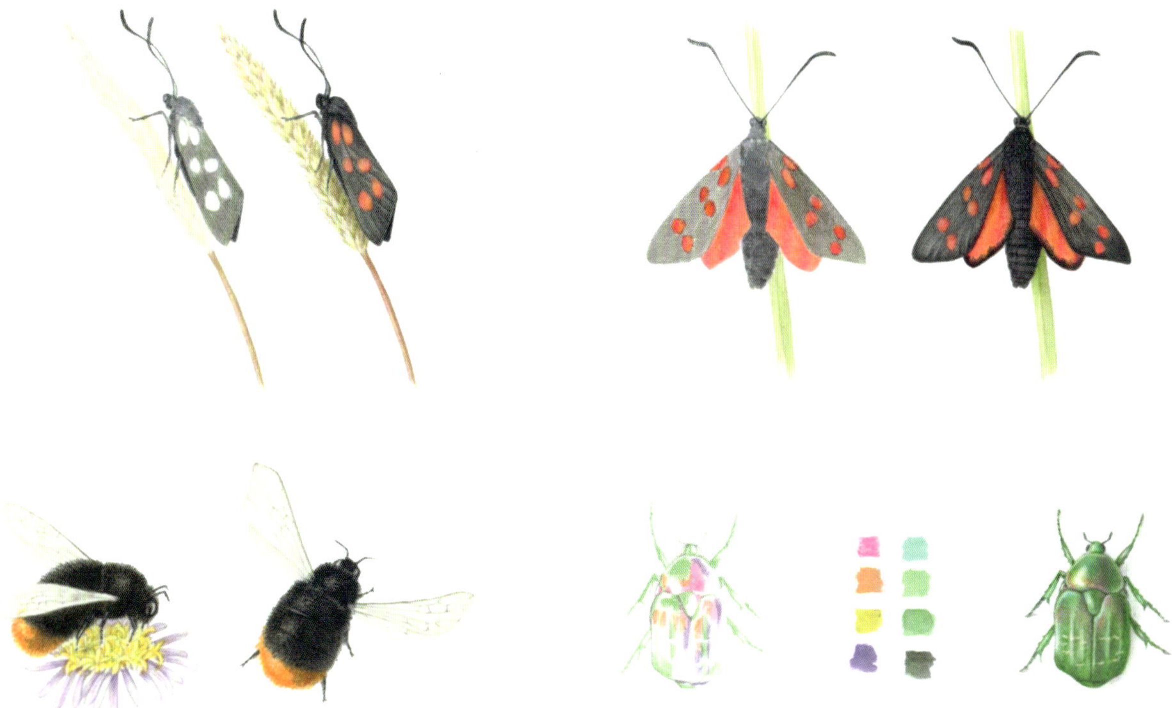

Painting

I usually use fine dry-brush stippling on top of a dry undercoat for the velvety texture of butterfly and moth wings. For hairy bumblebees, the dry brush-strokes are a little longer.

With iridescent beetles, I place different colours next to each other first, working with a dry brush and leaving clear highlights. I try not to move my head too much as that alters the colours and highlights. Then, when the paint is thoroughly dry, I apply fairly dry washes of the main colour, avoiding the highlights. Finally, a dry brush is used to crisp up the details.

Above: Burnet moths' wings have a slightly metallic sheen, so I used dark greenish undercoat washes. Dry brushwork strengthened the colours and sharpened the details.

Rose chafer and the – perhaps surprising – colours used to portray a green beetle.

Opposite page:
Pencil roughs of peacock, small tortoiseshell and common blue butterflies for a supermarket packaging illustration job and a wildlife trust project

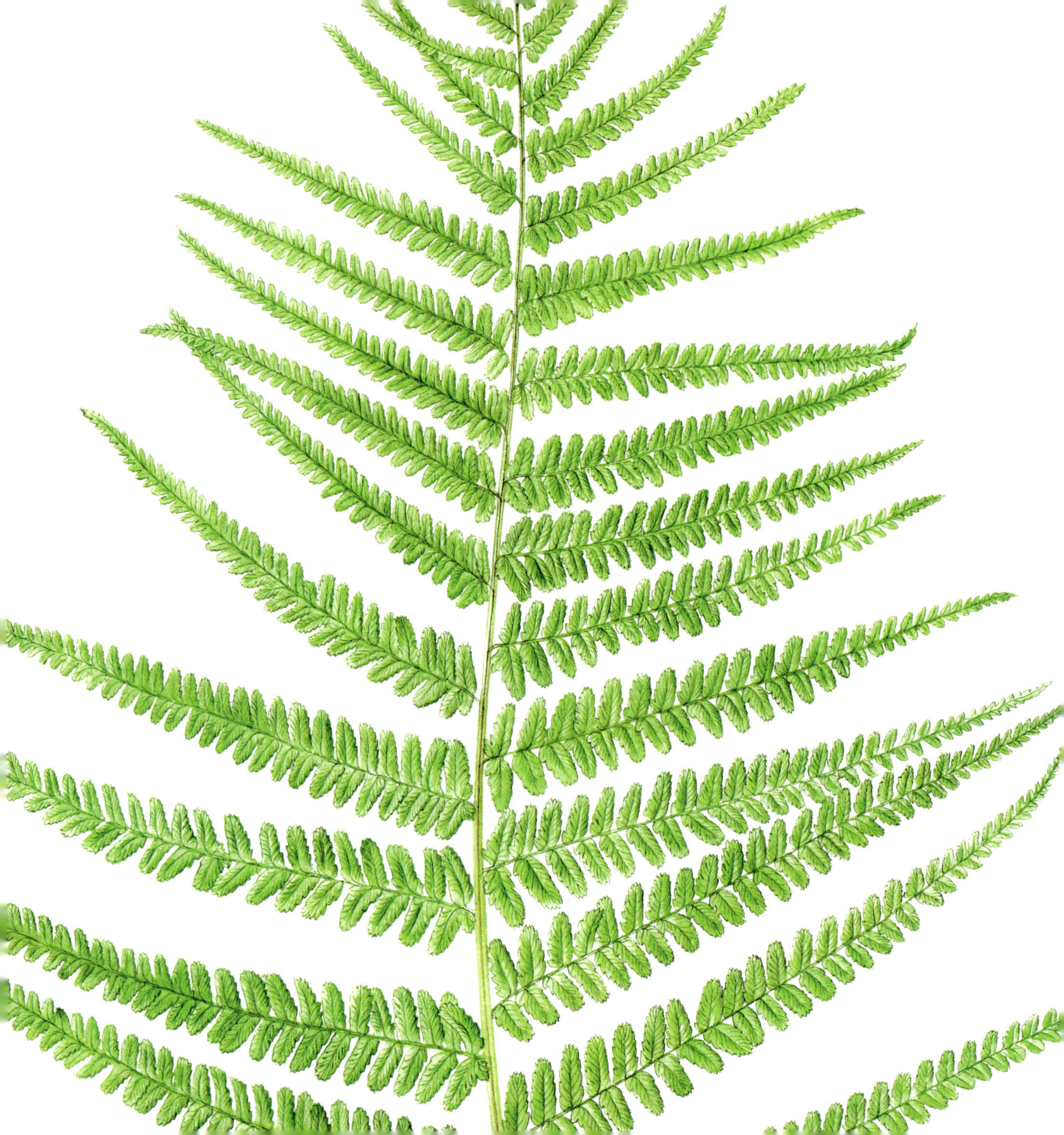

Section 4
'Lower' plants

'Lower' plants

'Lower' plants are those that reproduce by spores rather than by seeds, such as mosses, lichens and ferns, although the term seems rather dismissive for organisms that have thrived for millions of years, pre-dating flowering plants. Strictly speaking, fungi and lichens are not plants at all; but they are, of course, part of the whole story. However these organisms are classified, I love to study and paint them.

Like many botanical painters, I had often included little tufts of moss or lichen when I found them growing on the twigs I was painting but they became subjects in their own right for me when I was looking for a theme to paint for an RHS exhibit the early 1980s. I needed something that would flourish in the winter, when I was not too busy with other work. Once I started studying these organisms, I became totally hooked. I showed four collections of mosses, liverworts and lichens at the RHS in the 1980s and 1990s and was awarded gold medals on each occasion. After not having shown for many years, I was awarded another gold medal in 2018 for a display of lichens at the RHS London Botanical Art Show.

Seaweeds are algae and not classified as plants, but to me they are still part of the whole story.

Opposite page:
Fungi are classified as a separate kingdom from those of plants or animals. These fungal fruiting bodies were all found growing at The Hillier Gardens in Hampshire.

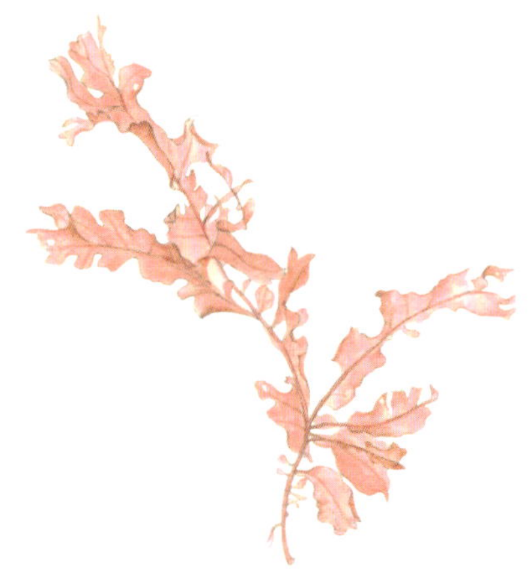

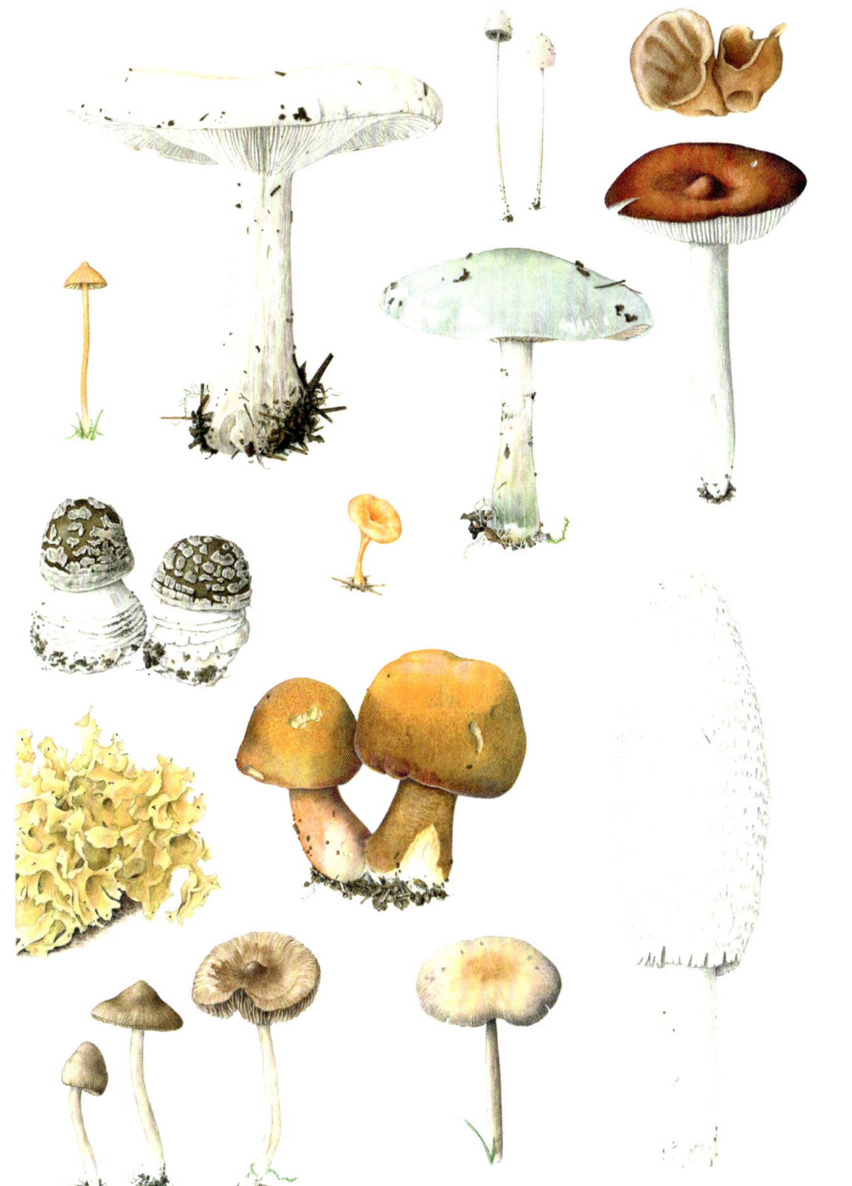

Lichens

When I discovered the wonderful world of lower plants, the lichens in particular stole my heart: their forms, colours and habits never cease to amaze me. Every lichen is in fact a symbiotic partnership between a fungus and an alga or cyanobacterium. Although by no means an expert, I am passionate about lichen and cannot resist pointing out these normally little-regarded organisms to everyone. I just love that moment when – having handed someone a lichen-encrusted twig and shown them how to use a hand-lens – I hear them gasp in astonished admiration.

Ramalina fastigiata and other lichens

What appealed to me about this branch was the variety of different species all growing together. Some were moved slightly to help the composition. This painting was a strong candidate for my 2018 RHS display, but I felt the large number of species it shows could be confusing. The different lichens demonstrate different types of apothecia, the spore-carrying bodies produced by the lichen's fungal partner. Some of the lichens growing flat on the twig have apothecia with margins, looking like tiny jam tarts. Others have apothecia with no margins. *Ramalina fastigiata* carries its apothecia at the tips of its branches, which is characteristic of the species.

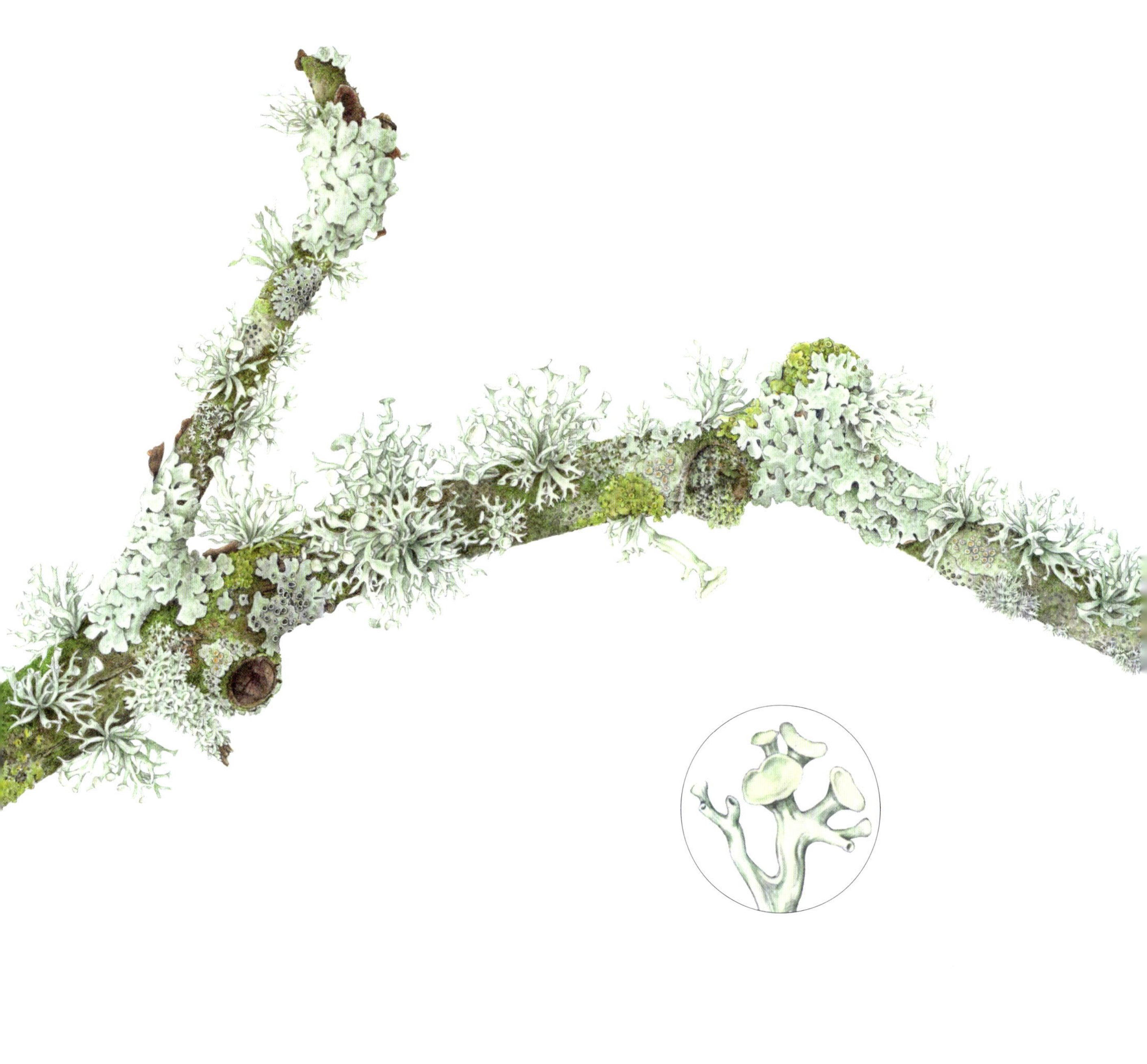

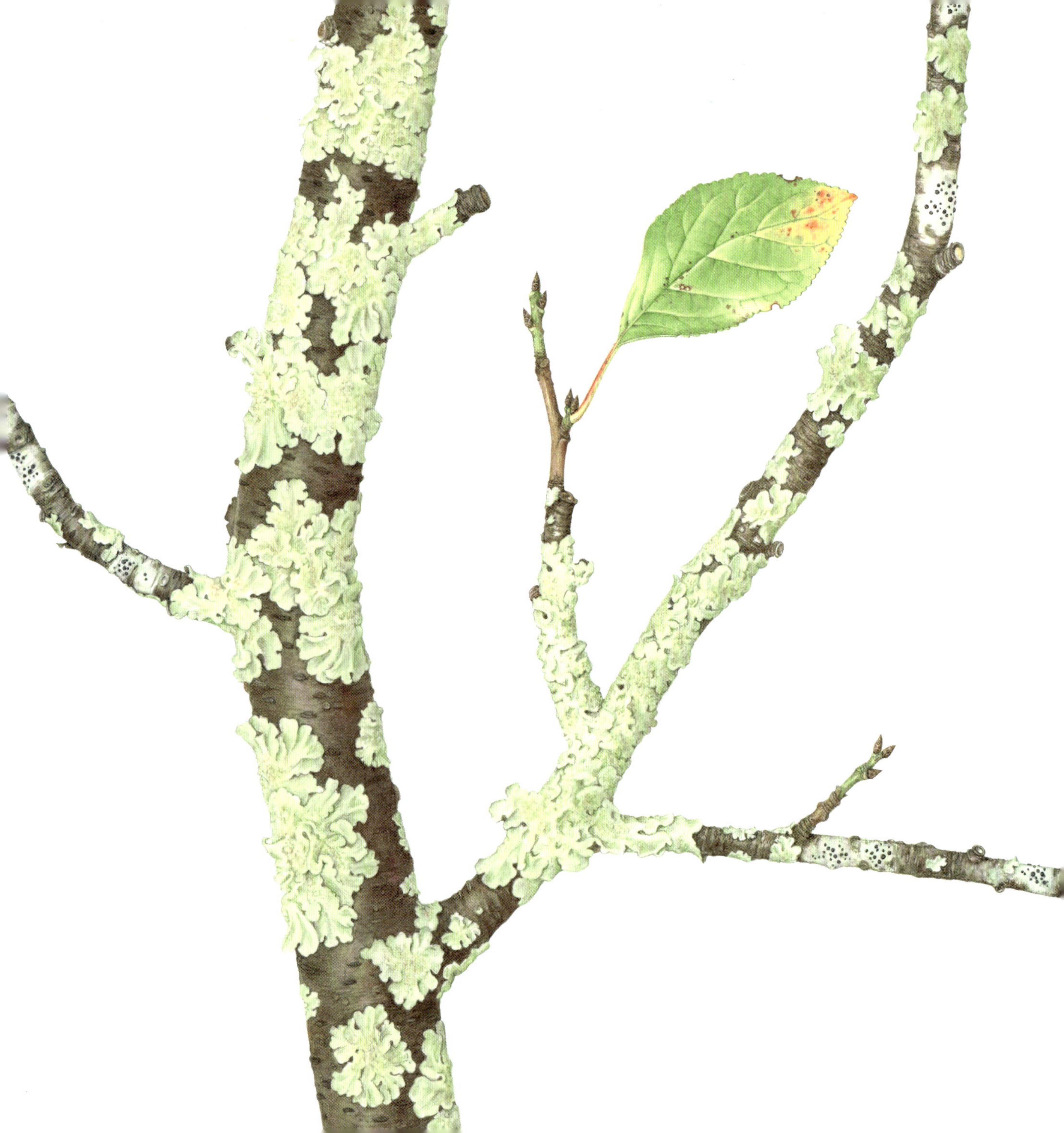

Flavoparmelia caperata

I wanted to show a little more of the tree on which this lichen grows and decided to include a leaf. As this was another possible candidate for my 2018 RHS display, I took great care with the composition. The lichened branches were painted first, then scanned and printed. I drew the leaf in various places on the prints before settling on the final composition.

When concentrating on painting the lichens, it is all too easy to forget that the twig and the lichens need to look cylindrical. I look out for tonal changes to help with this.

Usnea rubicunda, also known as *Usnea rubiginea*. This striking fruticose lichen does occur in some western parts of Britain, but the specimen shown here was found in Madeira.

Opposite page:
Flavoparmelia caperata on the plum tree

Evernia prunastri

I included this painting in my 2018 RHS display because it shows one of my favourite lichens. *Evernia prunastri* is easy to identify, as the underside of its branches is white. It looks like a fruticose (shrubby) lichen but is in fact a foliose (leafy) one, with exceptionally long, erect lobes. Fruticose lichens are the same colour on both sides.

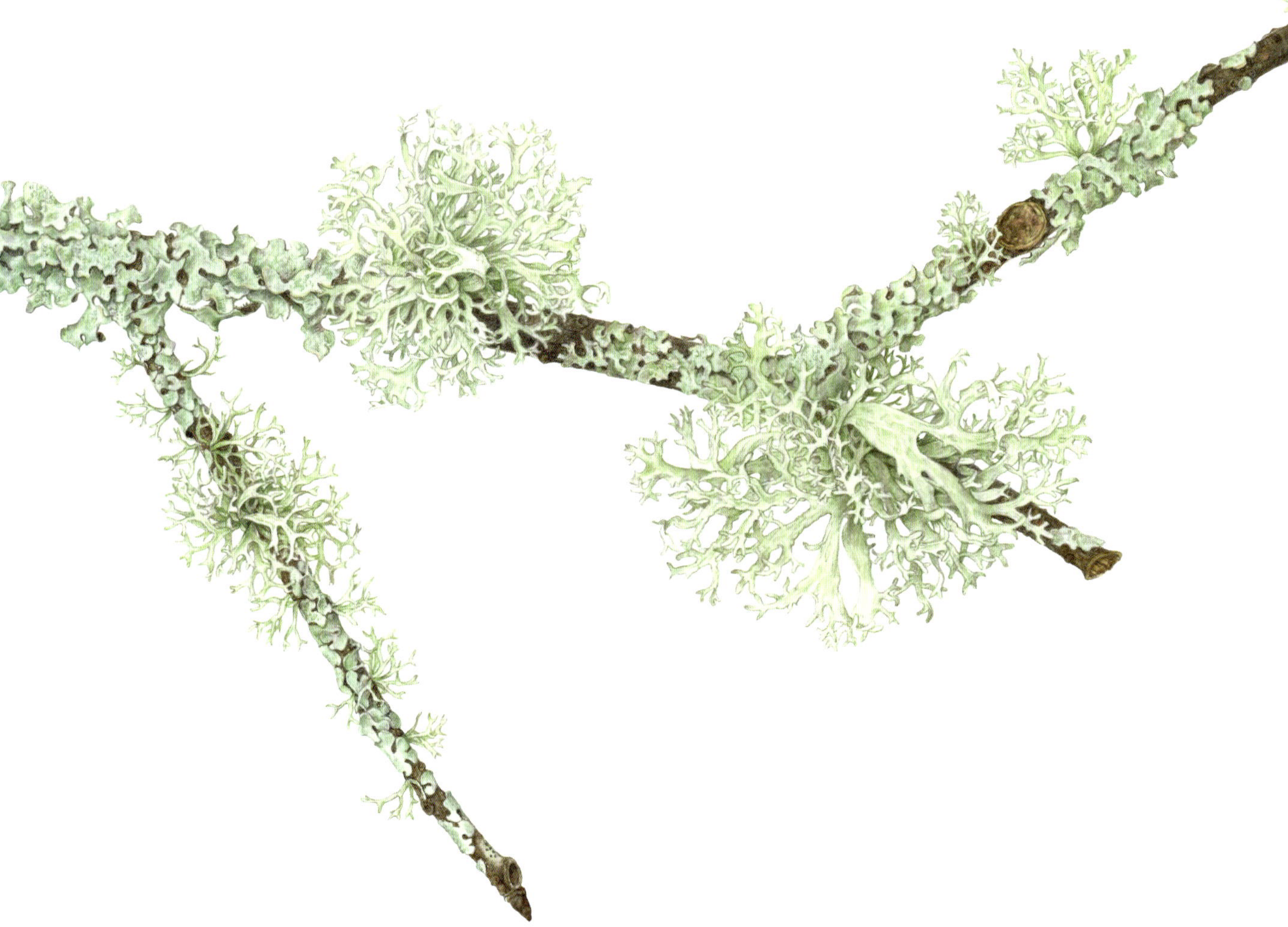

Left to right: Crustose (crusty), fruticose
(shrubby) and foliose (leafy) lichens

Opposite page:
Evernia prunastri, RHS London Botanical
Art Show 2018

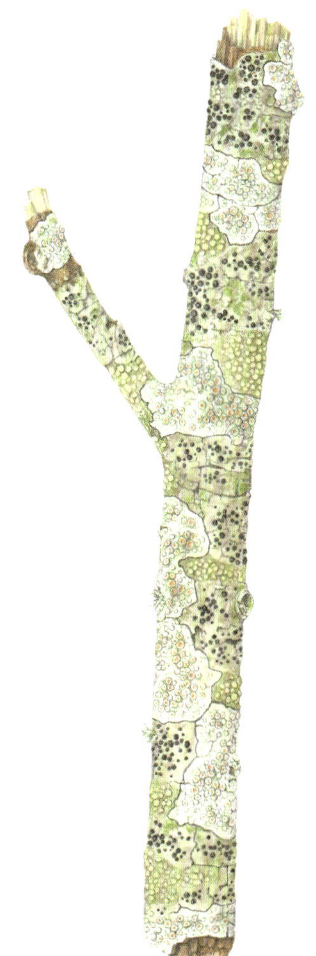

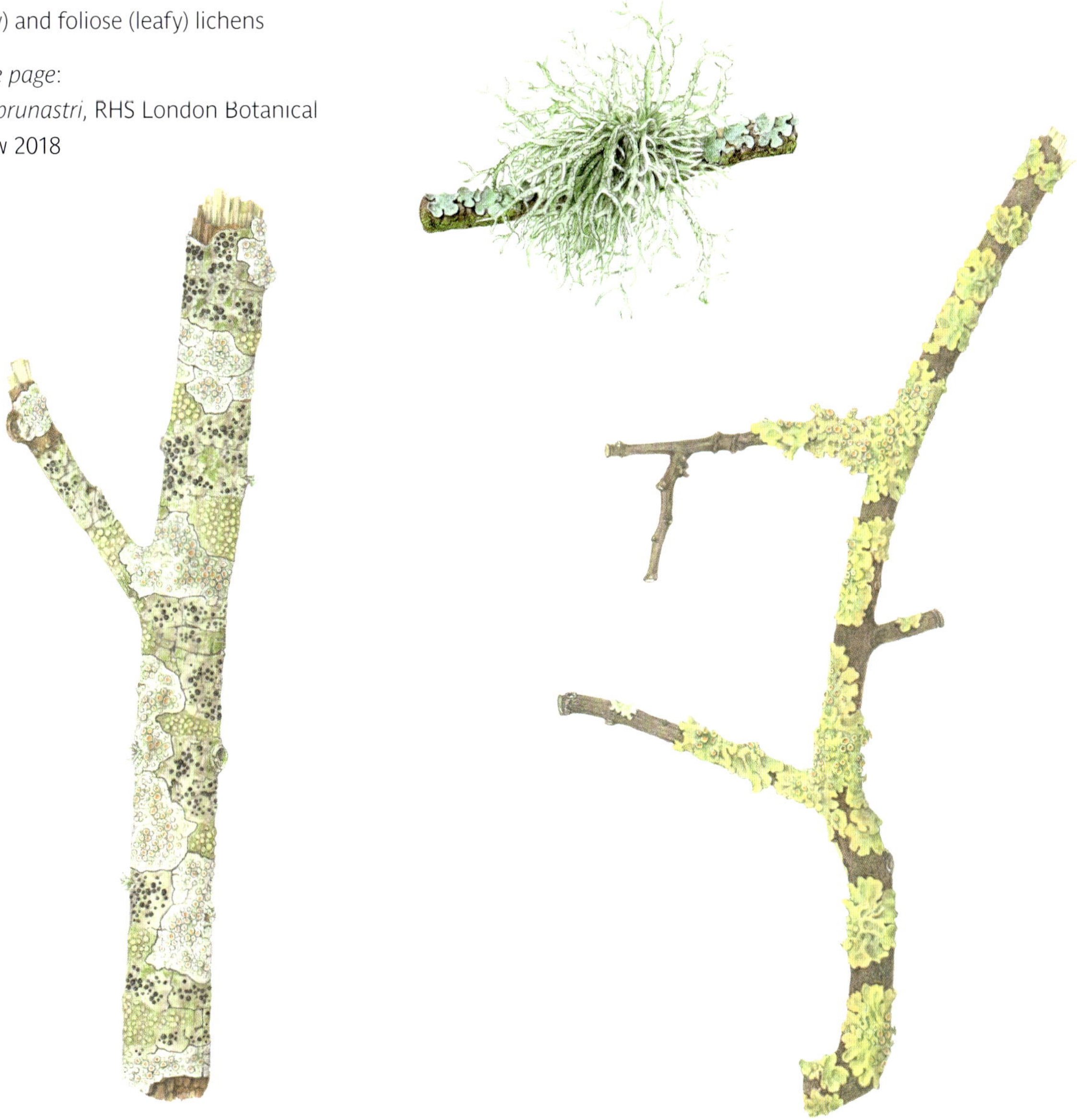

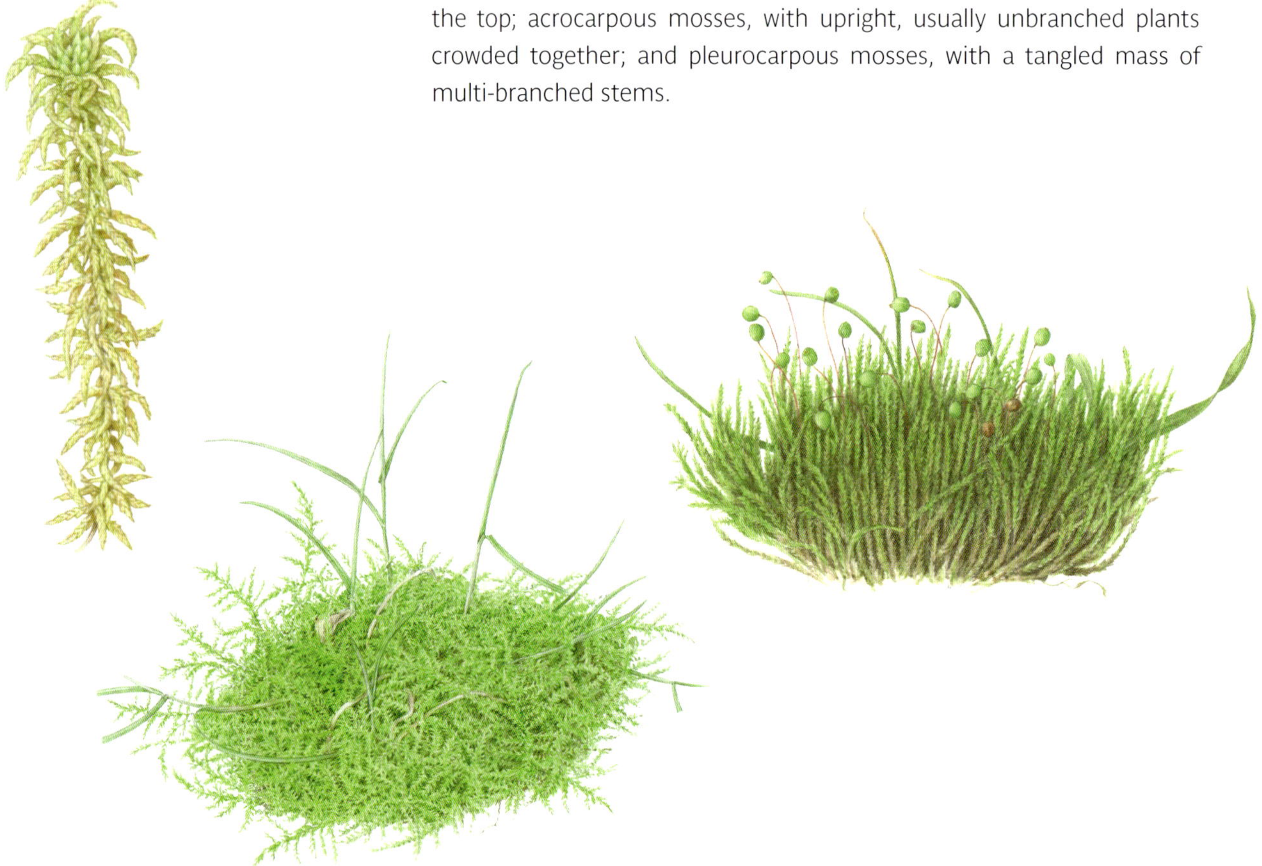

Left to right:

Sphagnum auriculatum, painted for an FSC identification leaflet

Kindbergia praelonga, a pleurocarpous moss

Philonotis fontana, an acrocarpous moss

Bryophytes

'Bryophyte' is the umbrella term for mosses and liverworts. They tend to flourish in damp places because they need moisture to assist in their reproduction. Identifying bryophytes usually requires a microscope or at least a strong hand-lens, and I love the miniature forests and jungles revealed under magnification. I study them under the lens to identify them and observe their structure, then paint them life-size without the lens.

Roughly speaking, there are three types of moss: bog-mosses or sphagnums, with branches in whorls up the stem and in a crowded tuft at the top; acrocarpous mosses, with upright, usually unbranched plants crowded together; and pleurocarpous mosses, with a tangled mass of multi-branched stems.

Atrichum undulatum

This large moss is quite common and makes extensive patches. My specimen came from a friend's woodland garden and I dug it up soil and all. It dried up quite quickly in the studio, so I sprayed it with water throughout the day and put it outside overnight. Mosses generally survive short periods of drought quite well and perk up once cooler, moister conditions return. This painting was part of my RHS display in 1986. The dead leaves hint at its habitat.

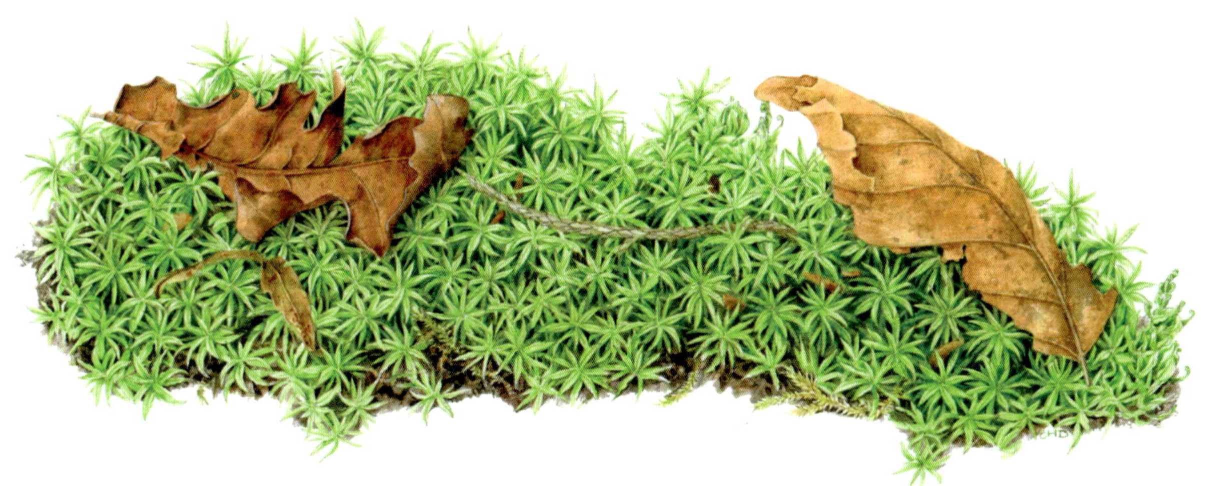

Liverwort *Lunularia cruciata*
with mosses

Lunularia cruciata

The scientific name comes from the moon-shaped cups on this liver-wort's surface. Asexual reproduction occurs when raindrops cause tiny gemmae to fall out of the cups and grow into new plants.

This type of liverwort flourishes in damp shade and I sometimes buy plants from garden centres just for the beautiful liverworts growing in their pots.

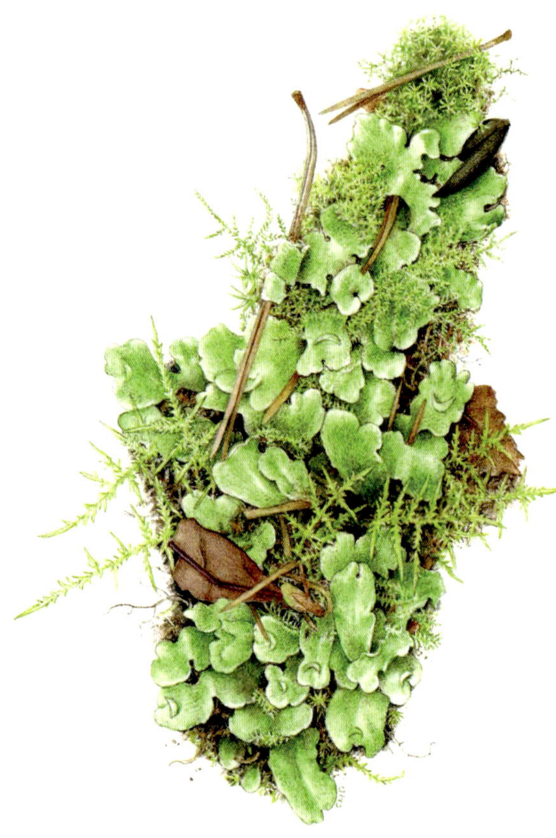

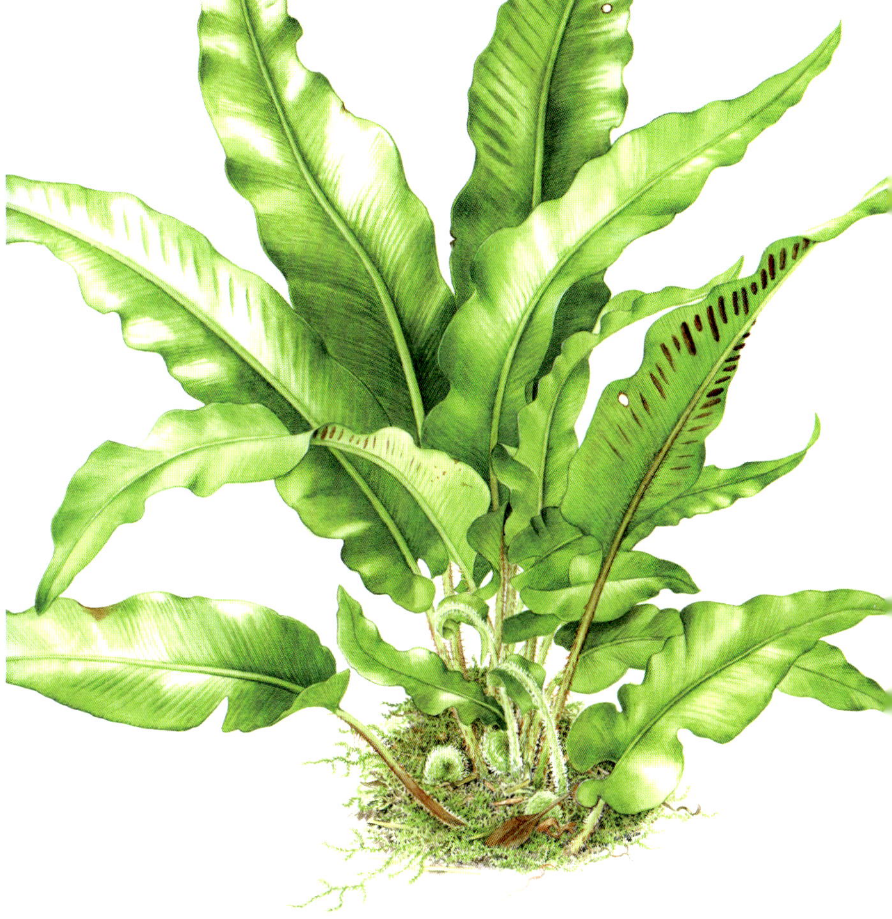

Hart's tongue fern,
Asplenium scolopendrium

Pteridophytes (ferns)

Ferns are plants that flourish in shady, damp habitats. At one time they were considered magical because their reproduction was mysterious, without obvious seeds. It was believed that, if found, fern seeds would make you invisible. In fact, ferns reproduce from spores carried in structures called sori on the underside of their leaves, and the shape and size of these sori can help to identify the species. In the 19th century ferns became extremely popular, and 'pteridomania' led to over-collection of some rare species.

Polypody on a mossy branch

Opposite page:
Male fern *Dryopteris filix-mas*

Polypody on a mossy branch

Some ferns grow epiphytically on the branches of trees, like this British polypody. They are not parasitic but simply use the tree to get better light. One of my students brought a piece of polypody with roots to a class to paint but did not want to keep it. I bound it to a log and covered it with moss, all held in place with wire and netting; kept well watered in a shady spot in my garden, it has flourished and grown. Now I can bring it into the studio any time. The Inside Story of painting this moss is shown on page 60.

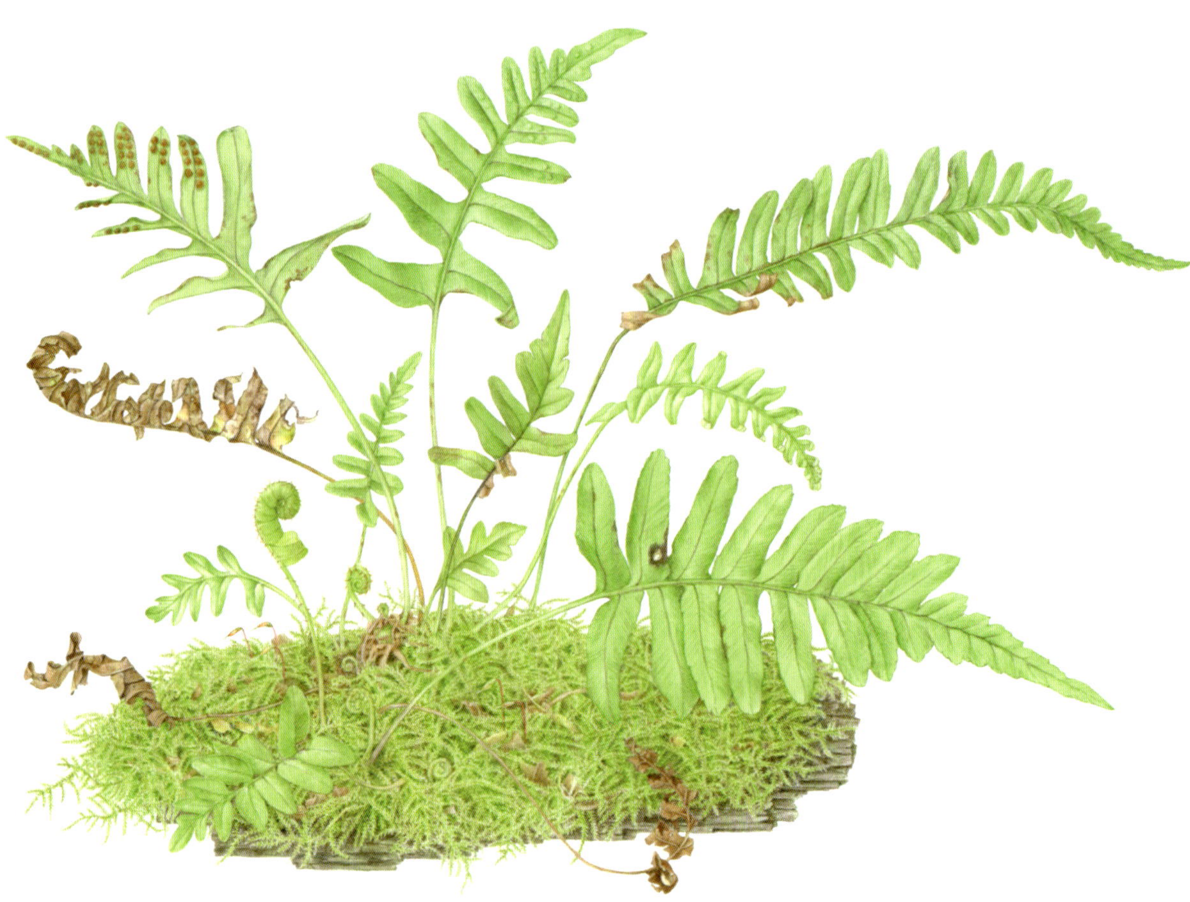

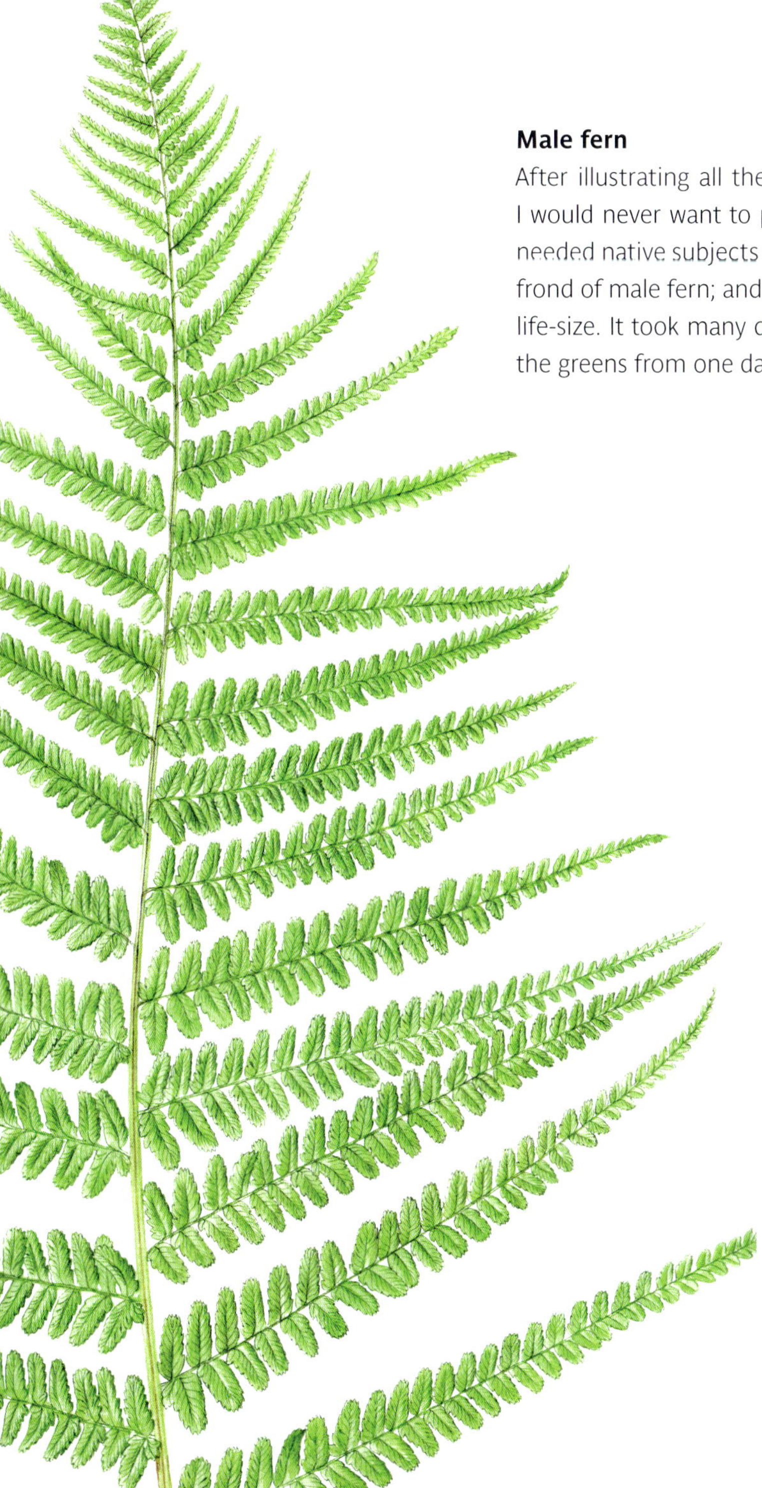

Male fern

After illustrating all the British ferns for *Collins Flower Guide*, I thought I would never want to paint one again – they were so fiddly. But when I needed native subjects for an exhibition, I couldn't resist this magnificent frond of male fern; and, unlike the illustrations for Collins, I could paint it life-size. It took many days to complete and it was a challenge to match the greens from one day to the next.

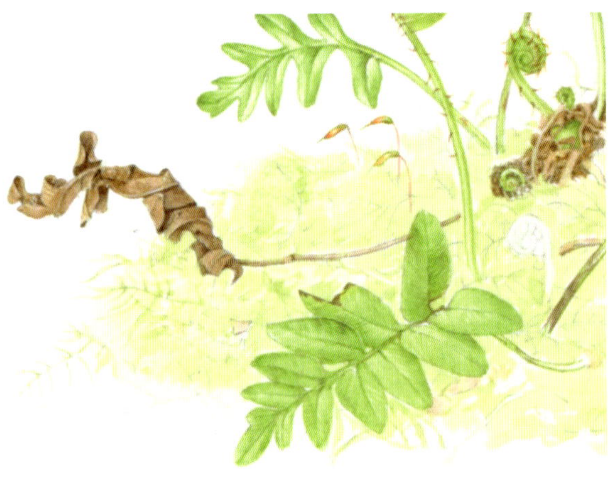

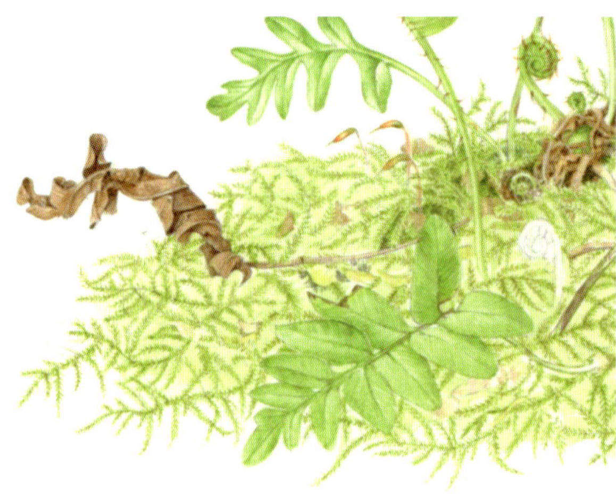

When I painted the moss *Kindbergia praelonga*, in the painting on page 58, I used the same process I employ when working on any kind of moss. The key points are the dryness of the paint, lightness of touch, good contrast and negative spaces on a very small scale. This moss took me about 24 hours of work, and the fern only slightly less.

Stage 1

The most obvious fronds of moss are indicated very lightly in pencil, with a single line. Then a pale green wash is applied over the whole area. This prevents any speckles of white paper showing in the finished work.

Stage 2

When the wash is dry, I paint in the pencilled fronds with a stronger green, the true moss colour. Having studied the moss under magnification, I can indicate the leaf shape and arrangement, using a fairly dry brush. I usually paint some branches against white at the edges to show their structure.

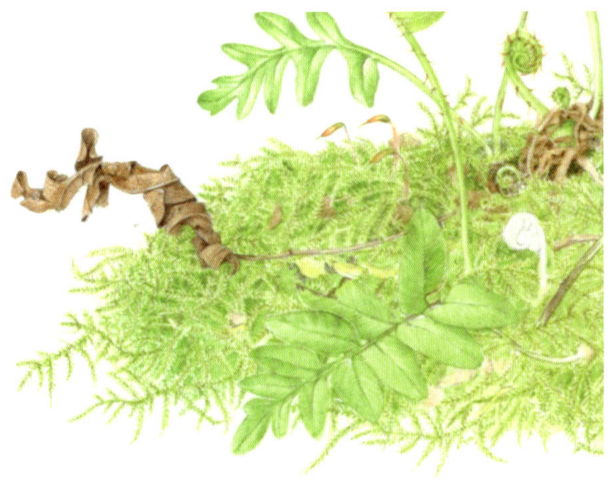

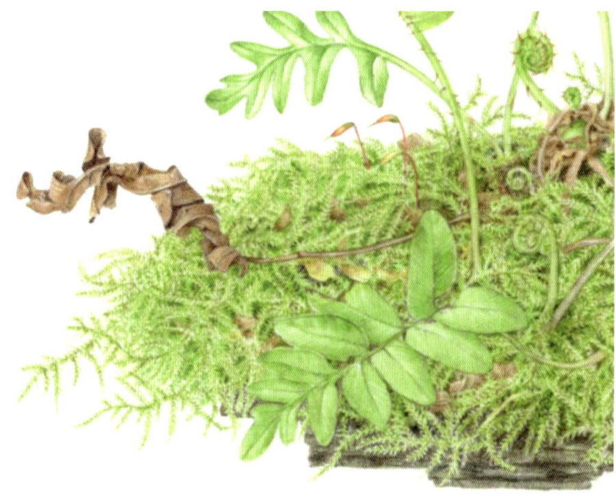

Stage 3

Now the hard work begins! With a darker, duller green I start to paint the negative spaces between the main branches. When I paint between the individual moss leaves, I try not to let them appear too regular.

Stage 4

I paint even smaller negative spaces with a darker green still, to suggest branches deeper within the clump. Some very tiny areas of 'serious dark' just here and there will give an impression of real depth. I usually mix these darks from colours used elsewhere in the painting, perhaps with an added touch of Perylene Green or Indigo. These final touches may need crisping up later, as paint tends to flatten itself into the paper over time.

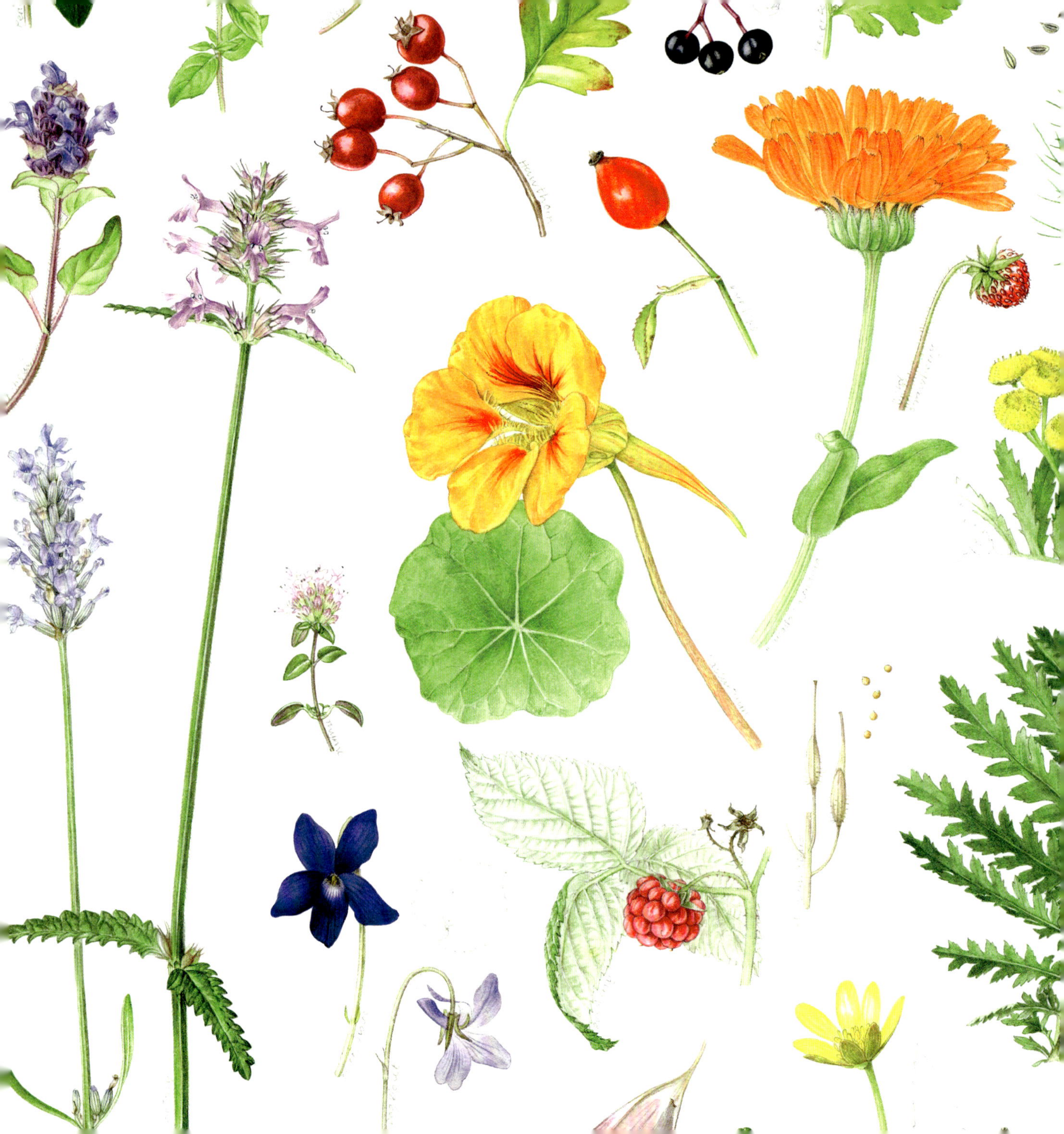

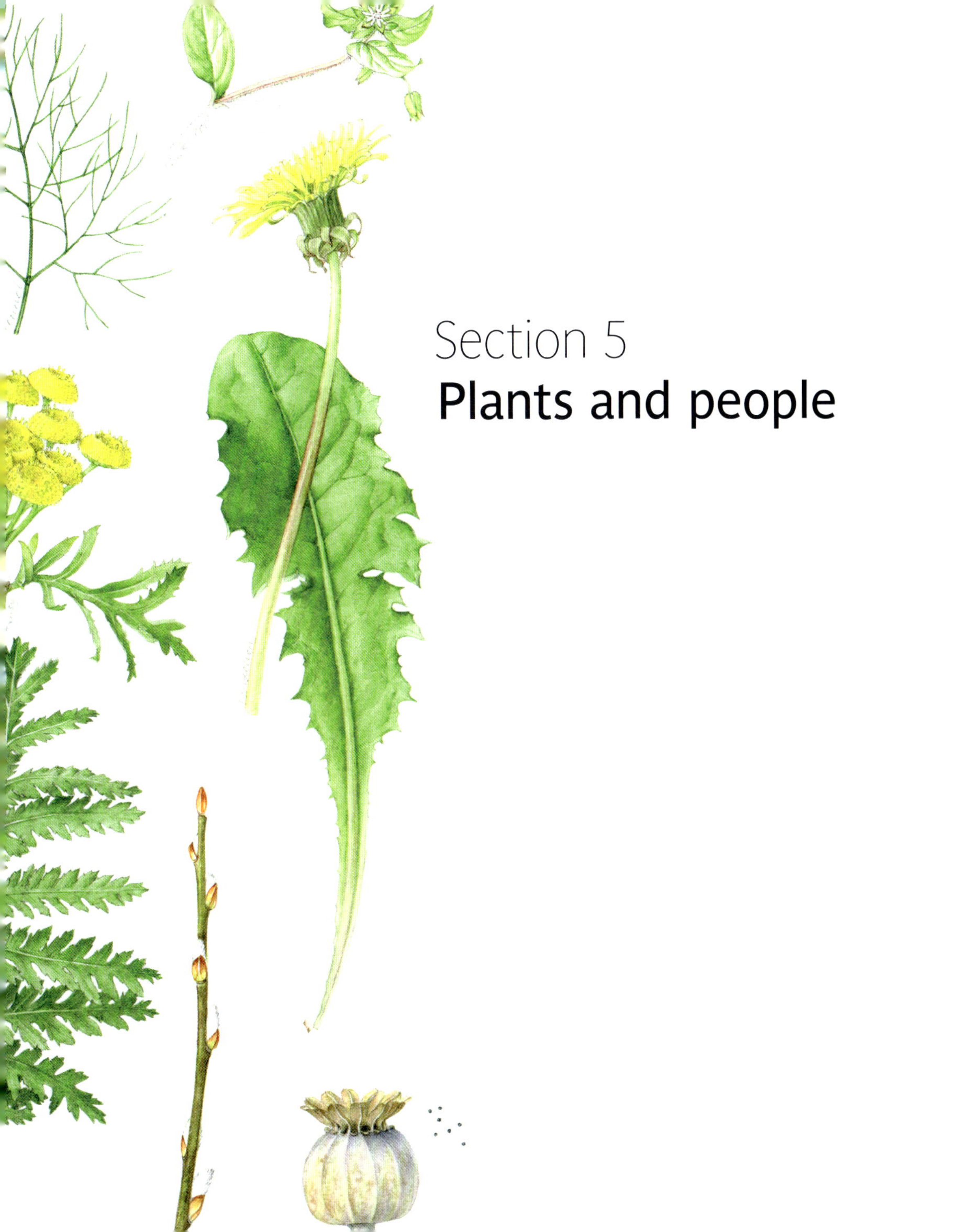

Section 5
Plants and people

Plants and people

Homes and gardens

The history of our interaction with plants is endlessly absorbing to me, ranking alongside the aesthetic and scientific aspects of my work. In my work I like to remind people of country walks, harvesting from the garden, or even our houseplants. We are surrounded by plants and have always depended on them, but as a society we are losing touch with nature and the seasons, and that alarms me.

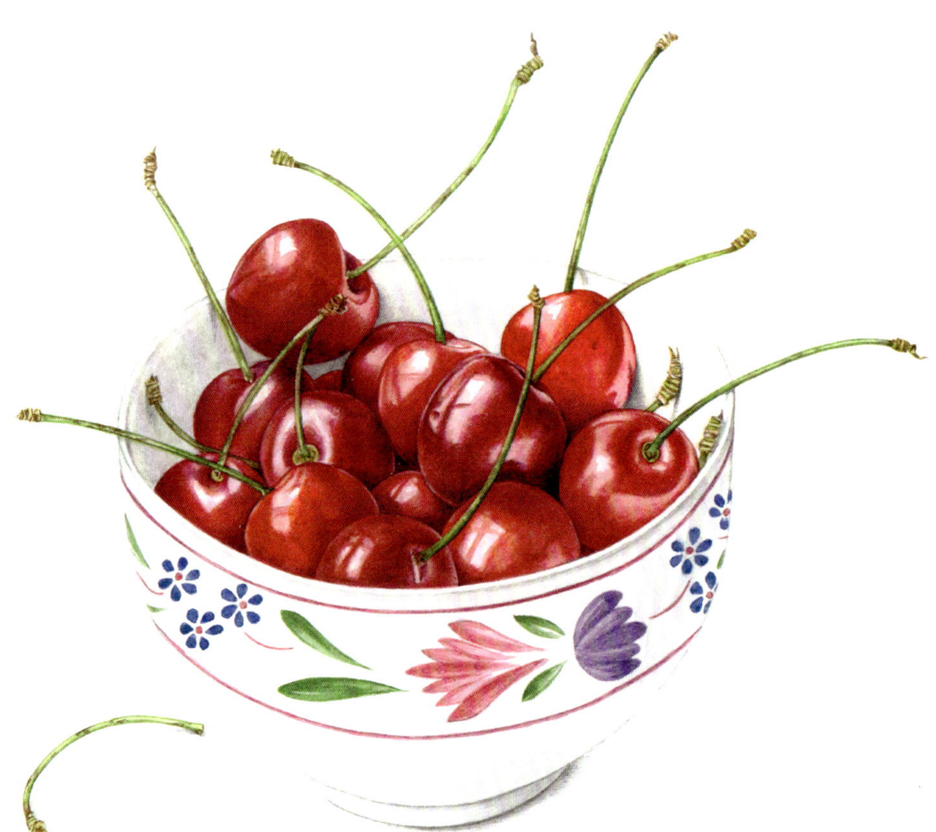

Life…
is just a bowl of cherries

Previous page:
My healing garden

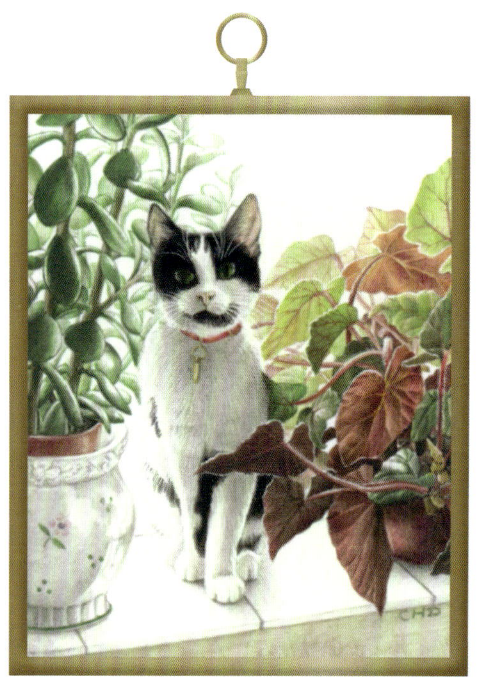

Ricky

This miniature of my cat Ricky among the houseplants is painted on vellum. I laid a light wash undercoat of an appropriate colour in each area and then built up detail and depth of colour in tiny strokes with the tip of a dry brush. There is a danger of spoiling the translucent effect of vellum by getting too much pigment on the surface; my students are always amazed how little paint is needed on the brush, and how little water.

The white hairs on the edges of the leaves were scraped out with the point of a sharp scalpel, as were Ricky's whiskers.

Ricky. Watercolour on vellum, actual size

Winter posy, Spring posy,
Summer posy

Opposite page:
Autumn posy

Seasons posies

This series of four paintings was made for a solo exhibition in 2016 on the theme of wild flowers.

Many people are afraid to pick any wild flowers as they think – wrongly – that it is illegal. This is really sad. Of course I do not advocate the reckless over-collection of plants, especially of uncommon species, and there are laws about this. (There is a downloadable Code of Conduct available at the Botanical Society of Britain and Ireland website: www.bsbi.org.uk.) But picking a *small* bunch of *common* and *abundant* flowers is not illegal, does no harm and, crucially, keeps us and our children in touch with our botanical heritage. I hope this is what these paintings convey.

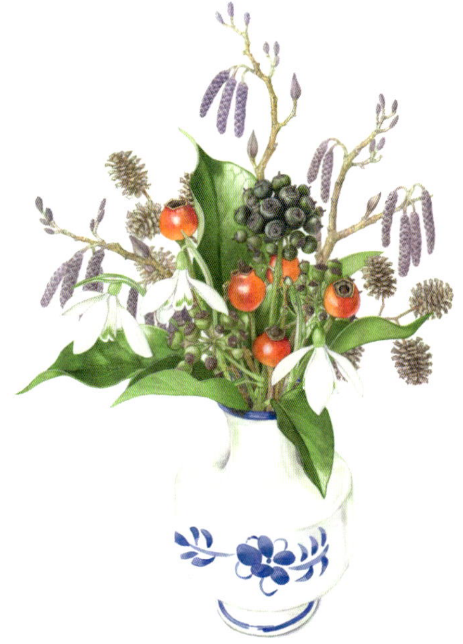

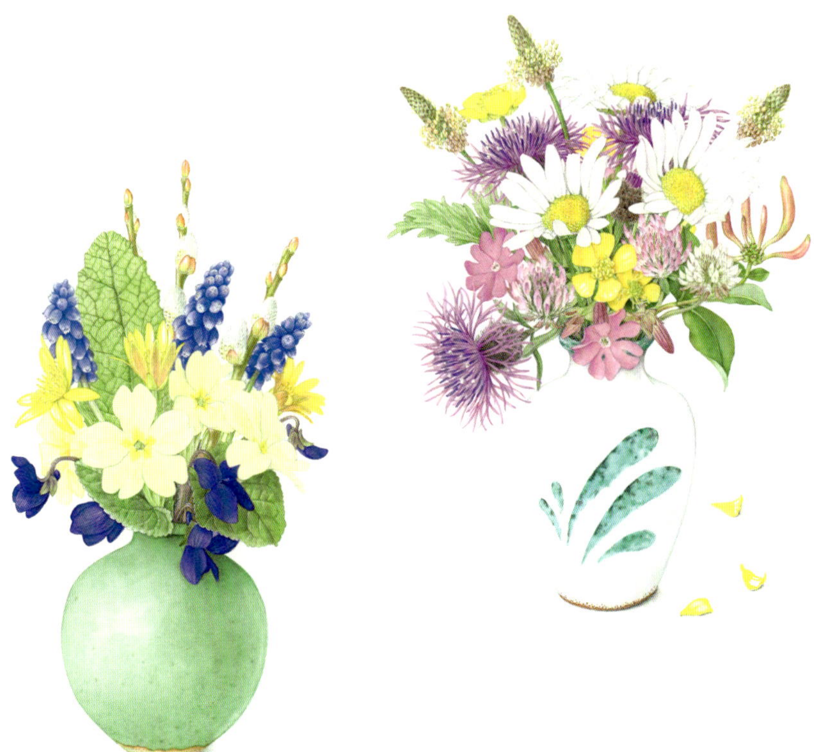

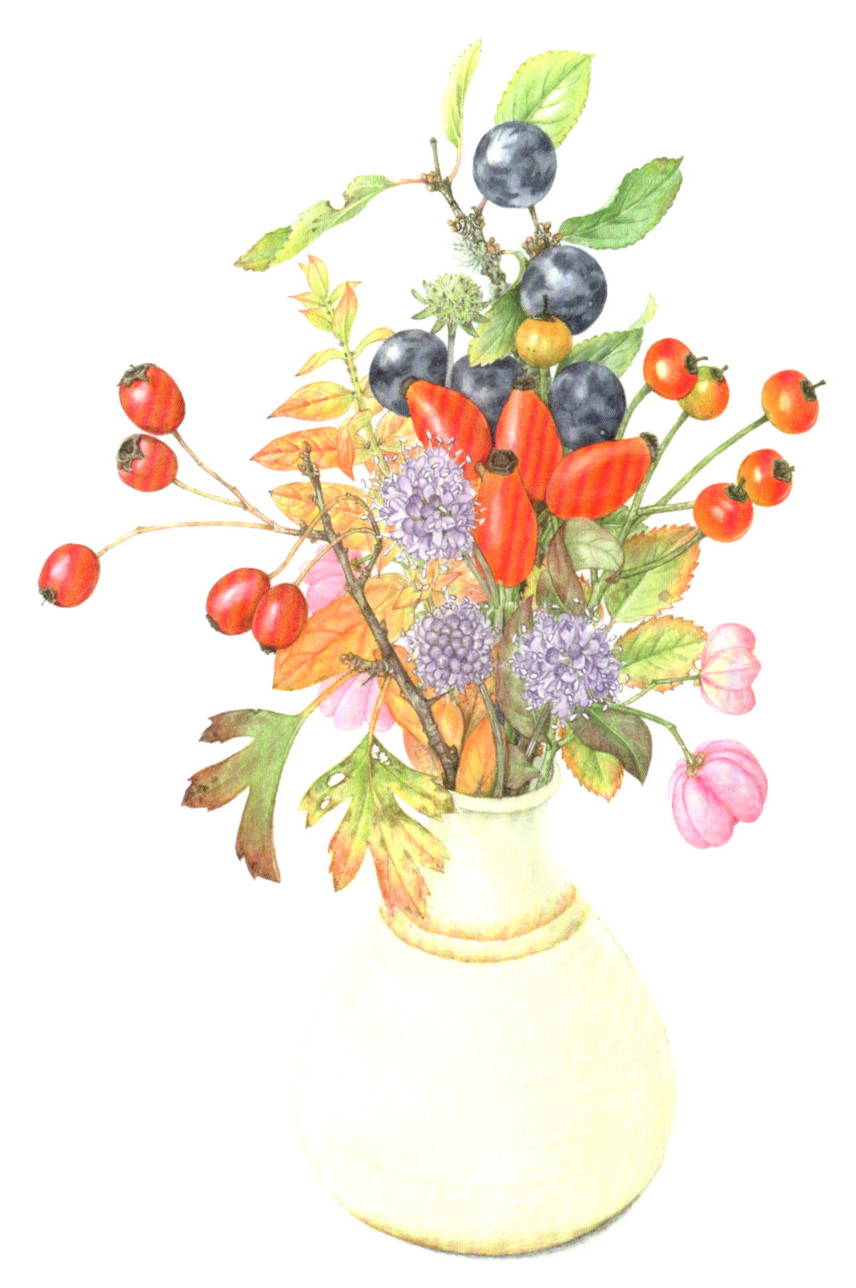

Senna pods were a famous, though rather harsh, remedy for constipation. From *Grandmother's Simples*, written with Elizabeth Smail, 2012

Opposite page:
Tisane de Quatre Fleurs

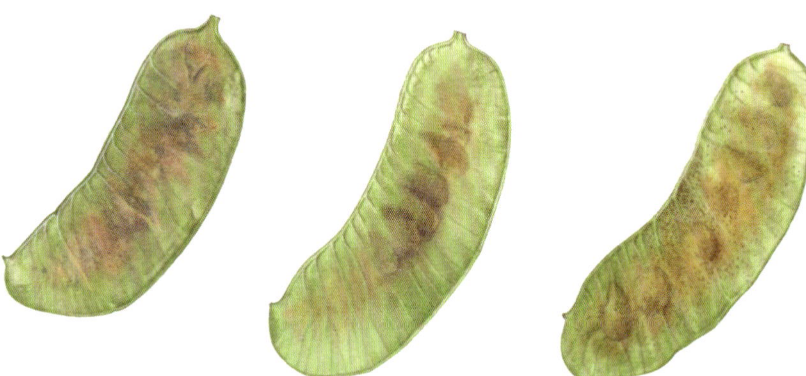

Herbal medicine

Humans have a long tradition of using plants as medicine – the only option before scientific medicine was developed. But even many modern drugs originated from plants, and we still take peppermint to settle the digestion or rub arnica on a bruise. Study of these old remedies is another of my passions, and I love the way it connects me with previous generations. I'm fortunate to have been asked to illustrate several herbals.

Tisane de Quatre Fleurs
This tisane (herbal infusion) from France was supposed to relieve the symptoms of flu. I included the slightly tattered paper to suggest the idea of traditional remedies being handed down through generations.

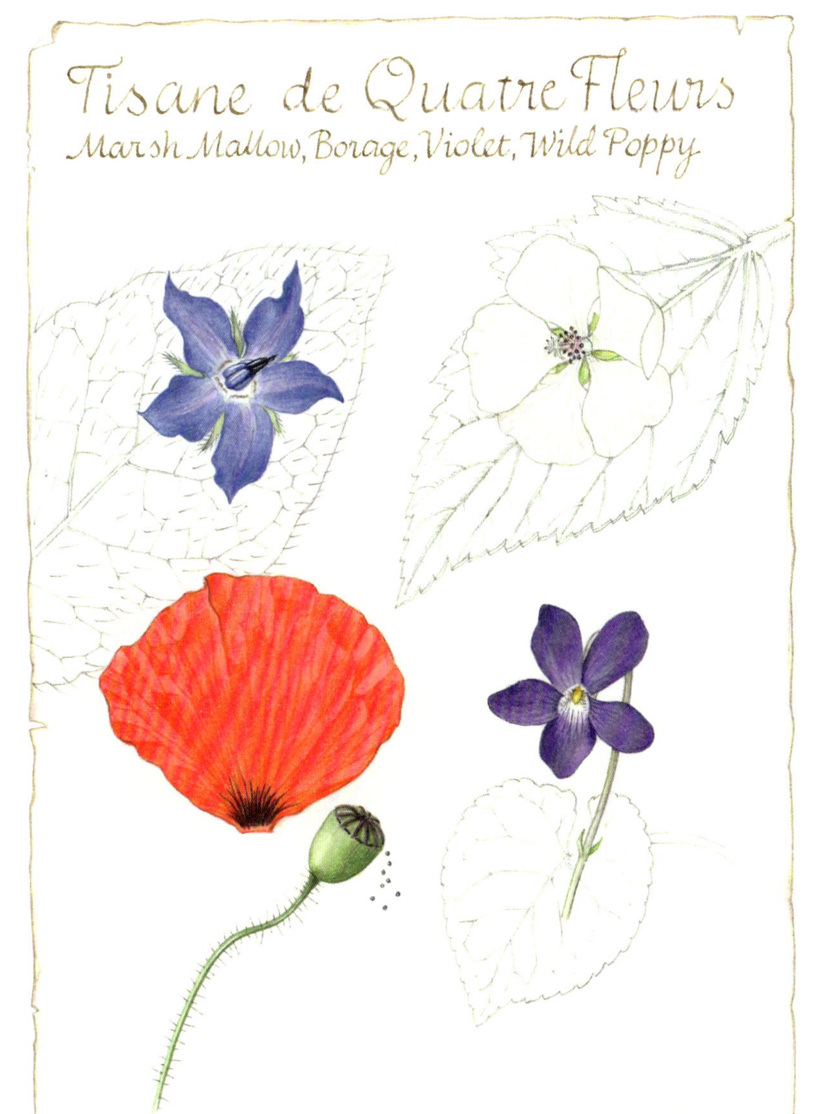

Tisane de Quatre Fleurs
Marsh Mallow, Borage, Violet, Wild Poppy

History, tradition and folklore

I have a love of history: not the kind defined by kings, queens, rulers and generals of the past (important though they were), but the history of the ordinary people. What were their lives like? What did they do, eat, think, believe? How did they entertain themselves? What stories did they tell? What did plants mean to them?

We have been using plants for food, medicine and myriad other practical purposes. We have also woven stories about them, and they are a part of our traditions. I love showing all this in my work – yet another aspect of the whole story.

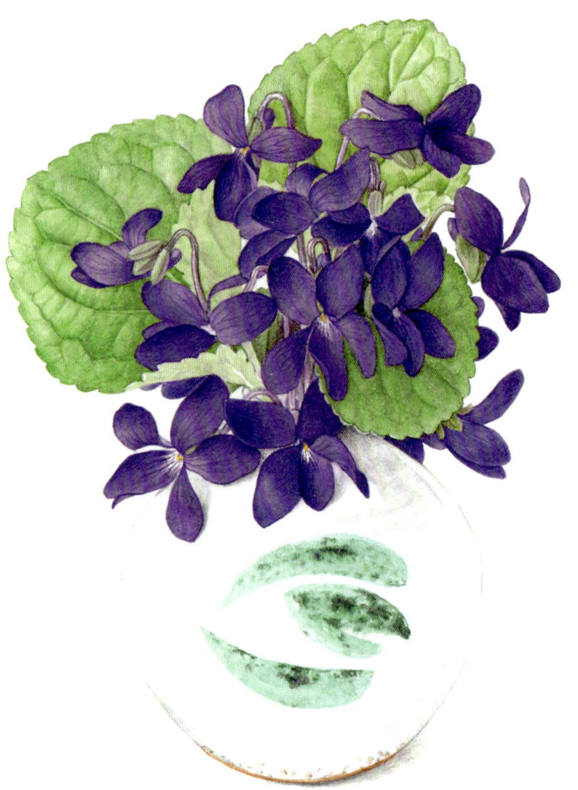

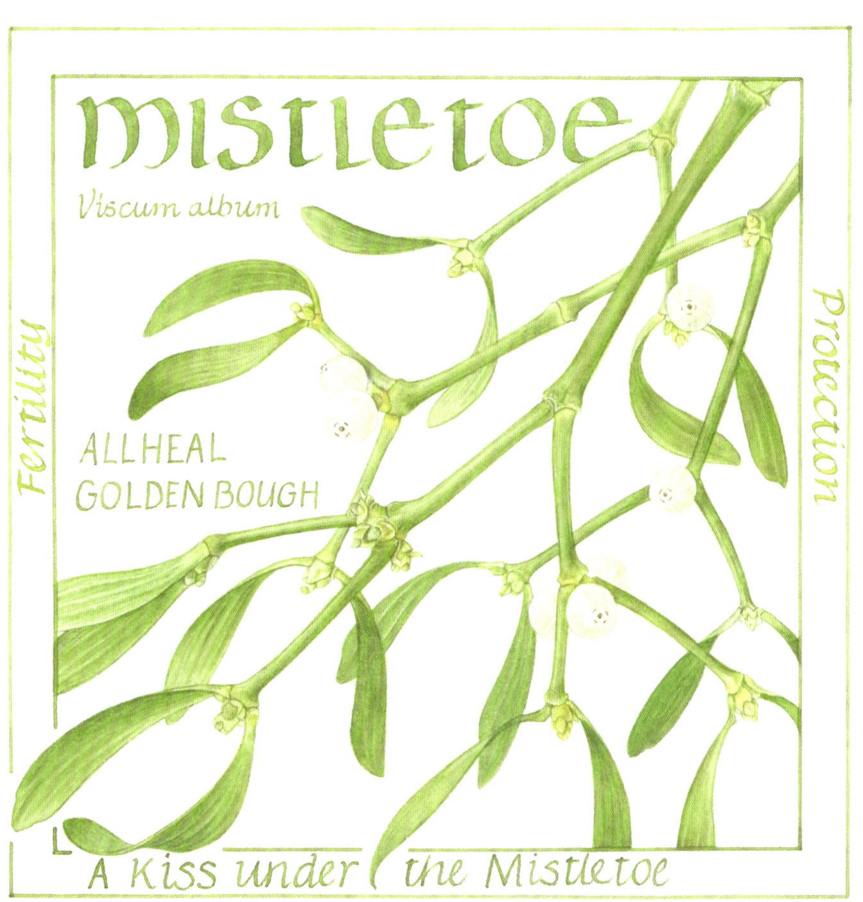

Mistletoe
Viscum album
Fertility
Protection
ALL HEAL
GOLDEN BOUGH
A Kiss under the Mistletoe

A Wild Plant Year

Collins Flower Guide was followed by another book about British wild plants, this time not a field guide, but a celebration of our long association with the native flora of Britain. I would write and illustrate it, using a slightly different style from an identification guide. Here, at last, was a chance to combine scientific accuracy with aesthetic considerations while also bringing in the historical, cultural and folklore dimensions of Britain's flora.

The images I made for this book are, by my own definition, not true illustrations: their primary purpose is so much more than to explain the plants. The paintings were also going to be for sale at the launch exhibition, so they had to work as exhibition pieces as well as on the page. Art *and* illustration! In my second book, *The Greenwood Trees*, I sometimes resolved this dual purpose by making large exhibition paintings and using details of these in the book. An example of this is the oak painting on page 27.

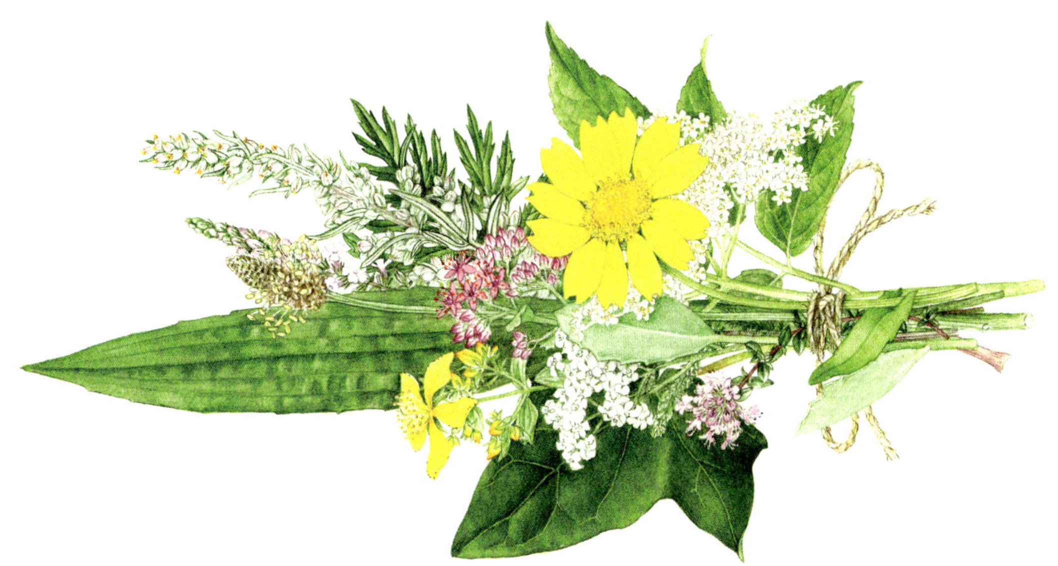

Christmas treats

Our Christmas celebrations still carry echoes of more pagan ways of marking the darkest time of year. I wanted to include evergreens – a symbol of everlasting life – together with more recent traditional elements such as the nuts, spices and fruits that are part of the Christmas feast.

The painting became an exercise in composition and also offered the challenge of several different surface textures. I had always intended to include lettering; winding it sinuously through the painting ties the elements together while suggesting festive ribbons.

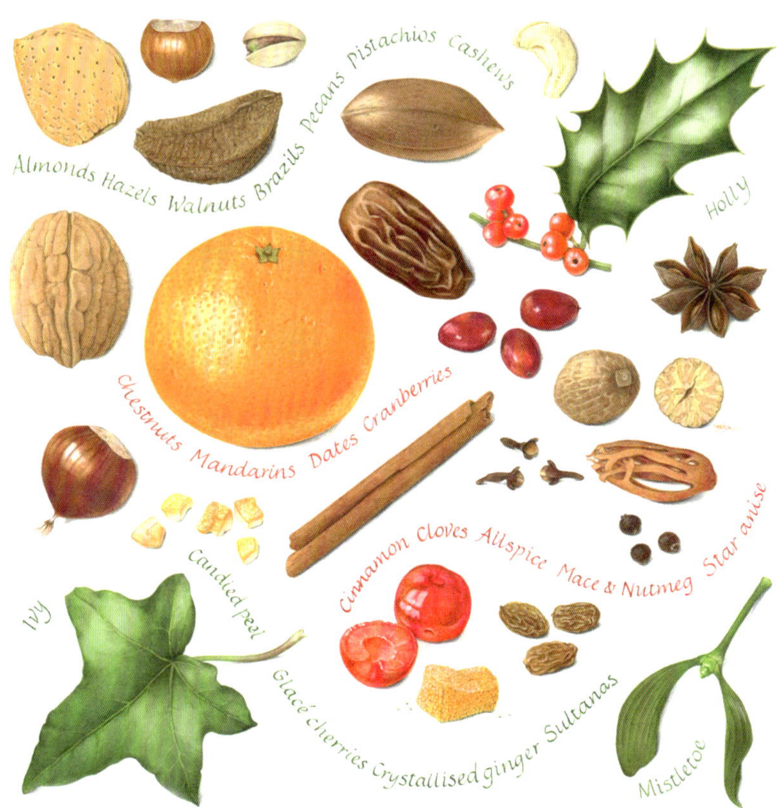

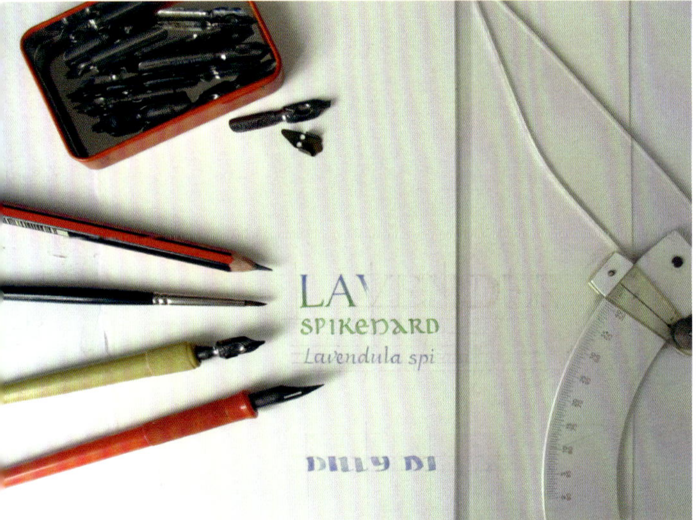

The tools I use for painted capitals and pen lettering

Lettering enables me to say something about the history and folklore I love, but I am no expert at calligraphy. I do lots of practice and then write all my inscriptions while 'in the zone', and I use a variety of lettering styles to suit the context. Any inscription, even a signature, is a compositional element, so it is essential to write it out on tracing paper first and then see where it fits best on the painting.

When preparing to write an inscription, I rule two lines that mark the height of a lower-case letter x, with lines above and below for ascenders and descenders (the parts of letters that extend above the x height or below the baseline). Every inch or so, I mark a vertical line (or, for italic, a 15 degree forward slope), to help keep my lettering uniform. Then I lightly pencil the inscription in place. I generally paint all-capital inscriptions with a brush, while other styles are written with either a slant-edged calligraphy nib or an ordinary dip-pen. Rather than ink I use watercolour, transferred to the pen with a brush.

The Holly & the Ivy

With this painting, based on the traditional Christmas carol, I originally had the ampersand (the 'and' sign) on its own in the top right-hand corner – but it looked wrong. Luckily there was room in front of 'the Ivy', so I lifted it out with a damp brush and a clean blotter, painted another ivy leaf in its place and wrote a new ampersand at the bottom. The finished painting hung in an exhibition in Winchester Cathedral and the plant conservation charity Plantlife used it for their 2018 Christmas card.

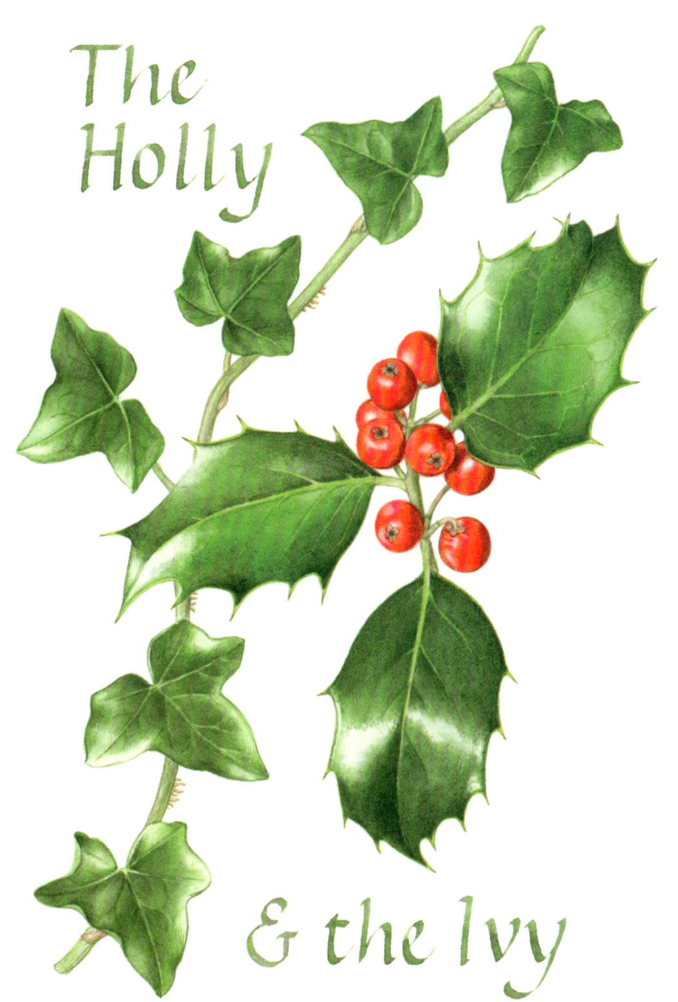

The
Holly
& the Ivy

Two Rivers Press has been publishing in and about Reading since 1994.
Founded by the artist Peter Hay (1951–2003), the press continues
to delight readers, local and further afield, with its varied list
of individually designed, thought-provoking books.

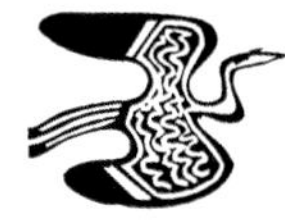